BLACK WALLS
AND OTHER STORIES

18

BLACK WALLS
AND OTHER STORIES

by

LIU XINWU

edited by Don J. Cohn
with an introduction by Geremie Barmé

— An Authorized Translation —

A *RENDITIONS* Paperback

Renditions Paperbacks
are published by
The Research Centre for Translation
The Chinese University of Hong Kong

General Editors
Eva Hung   T.L. Tsim

Printed in Hong Kong

Contents

Contents

Introduction

by Geremie Barmé

On 19 May 1985, a soccer riot in Peking made headlines throughout the world. Liu Xinwu, a Cultural Revolution propagandist who developed into one of the most highly regarded official writers of the post-Mao period, gave us an account of the incident in the controversial story "Zooming in on 19 May". Four years to the day, on 19 May, 1989, Chinese Premier Li Peng declared peaceful student-led protests in Peking to be a "counter-revolutionary disturbance" and in accordance with the directions of the aged Deng Xiaoping and President Yang Shangkun deployed a massive force of troops to enter the city and "restore order". When the People's Liberation Army finally entered Beijing on 3-4 June the resultant massacre and the purge that followed in its wake changed the face of China's political and cultural life.

Liu, an interested bystander and supporter of the 1989 Protest Movement,[1] was collecting material on popular reactions to the student agitation before the massacre. Following the bloody

---

[1] The complex of student marches, popular demonstrations, petitions, strikes and samizdat publications during April–June 1989 is better seen as part of a massive process than simplistically, and I believe incorrectly, labelled as a "democracy movement".

repression of June Liu's official stock has suffered a sudden fall. But this is not the first time Liu has fallen prey to the political fiats of the Party; his writing career has often paralleled and reflected the turbulent ideological climate of contemporary China.

In the Cultural Revolution art and literature served the limited aims of political leaders who saw culture as little more than a weapon to be used in a seemingly endless round of purges. Liu Xinwu, a middle-school teacher who wrote fiction on the side, produced children's stories that promoted class struggle, calling on his jejune readers to inform on spies, class enemies and bad elements and to participate energetically in the lunatic politics of the day. Those clumsily-written works of political pedagogy were soon forgotten when, in the late 1970s, Liu began publishing stories about the dilemmas of young people, in particular Peking middle-school students, in popular journals, establishing himself as one of the most prominent writers of "scar" literature. While these stories accorded with the ascendant Party line rejecting the Cultural Revolution and its educational policies, Liu cloaked his new propaganda in the popular garb of fiction, and by the early 1980s, Liu was a major establishment author with a wide readership.

Official recognition and literary fame enabled Liu to embark on an intriguing and sometimes hazardous path. While never a reprobate or heretic in regard to current Party orthodoxy, over the past decade Liu has managed better than many other establishment writers, such as Jiang Zilong or Ru Zhijuan, to balance acceptability with outspokenness, obedience with honesty. While in the following stories we may not find the voice of an independent and original artist, we do encounter the careful diction of the sophisticated state artist who reveals his humanity and understanding of the world within the often fluid confines of Party dogma.

Writers like Liu Xinwu have been an important force in the

"reformist camp" of China's official cultural community. Like Wang Meng, novelist and ex-Culture Minister (Wang was relieved of his position in September 1989), Zhang Jie, Feng Jicai, Zhang Xianliang, Shen Rong and many others, Liu is a state employee, and his position as a public servant always circumscribes his independence. As Miklos Haraszti, the perceptive Hungarian critic of civilian (as opposed to military) socialist culture has written in his classic *The Velvet Prison: Artists Under State Socialism:*

> The professional writer knows that the right to speak carries with it responsibility. His writing must be not only beautiful but also useful: his care with these two aspects is what makes him a writer...
>
> Long gone are the days when artists waited, in happy or frightened ignorance, for successive instructions concerning speedy fulfilment of the five-year plan! Today every artist is a minor politician of culture. We prepare our innovations so as to bid competitively for the creation of an official aesthetic.[2]

Liu Xinwu has been a willing participant in the creation of the Chinese Velvet Prison, a structure built under the auspices of post-Mao reformist socialism in China. The Velvet Prison offers the compliant artist all the perks of the modern state — access to the media and literary journals, official recognition, travel in China and overseas and an assured income to go with it — and licence to be artistically innovative as long as he does not transgress the borders of orthodoxy. In the case of Liu Xinwu, the relative laxity of the past decade along with the pressures placed on writers by

---

[2] Miklos Haraszti, *The Velvet Prison: Artists Under State Socialism* (New York: Basic Books, 1987) p. 78.

the economic reforms and the need to make money has made it possible — or perhaps necessary — for Liu to experiment with new styles and themes in his writing.

Throughout the 1980s, Liu continued his observations of urban low life, especially of city youth. In this collection "Zooming in on 19 May" and "Bus Aria", both written in 1985, are examples of this abiding interest. Strictly speaking, the former belongs to the genre of reportage, that school of socialist New Journalism in which fact and fiction are combined in a narrative both to edify and entertain the reader. But in this particular piece, about a controversial soccer riot, some critics and political figures found that Liu had cut too close to the bone; he had crossed that fine line between constructive criticism and literary insolence.

While valiantly juggling many contentious themes in the story — foreign reporting on China and xenophobia, urban unrest and inflation, alienation among young people and official indifference, national pride and Ah Q-ism — to some critics Liu indulged in a little too much philosophizing and irresponsible commentary. He was reportedly criticized harshly for the story, in particular for raising the point that the riot was related to price rises in Peking. In fact, many of the issues touched on or discussed even cursorily in the story have gained a new relevance as a result of the events of 1989. One particular interjection by the author near the end of the piece is of interest in the light of the decision by China's elders to crush the protest movement in June:

> We need to be more rational in our responses; more notice should be taken of local reactions, in particular those of our own people, of our young people, regardless of whether they are direct or indirect, pleasing or offensive. If a country is constantly annoyed by its youth, concerned solely with lecturing them and never bothering

to listen to them, then that country is suffering from senility...

It has been suggested that "Bus Aria", a far less controversial work published later in 1985, was in fact written to balance out the "negative effect" of "Zooming in on 19 May". It is a work that starts out promisingly but has a forced and unnatural ending, but despite the lip service paid to social ideals by the old man who acts as the Party's *deus ex machina* in the narrative, the piece remains a readable fiction centring on an incident that takes place on one of Peking's overcrowded buses. Of course, the story may also be read as an allegory about Peking in general.

Liu is attracted in his fiction to the study of modern Peking Man. Many of his stories deal with the pressures, frustrations and hopelessness of life in Peking, the town in the city. "Black Walls" can be taken as a simple tale about life in the overcrowded courtyard tenements of the old city; equally, it can be seen as an extended metaphor about privacy, interfering street committees and individualism. "White Teeth", the most recent work in this collection, deals with the alienation a woman experiences at home, in her workplace and in love. The story has a veneer of the slightly absurdist humour that has been modish in Chinese literature since the mid-1980s. The reason that Liu fails to exploit fully the absurd possibilities of the situations in stories like "Black Walls" or "White Teeth" is, perhaps, because everyday life in China has such a strong absurdist aura that fiction can never do it justice. On the more mundane level is "The Woman with Shoulder-length Hair". A writer like Saki might have made it a dark and mordant story; Liu produces a sweet-sour concoction with a twist in the tail.

The 1980s has seen the revival and growth of a school of Peking fiction, the *Jingwei xiaoshuo*, or "Peking novel", as it is called in Chinese. Lao She (1899–1966) was the master of this genre and such novels as *Rickshaw Boy* and *Old Zhang's Philosophy* are regarded as important works of this genre. His 1957 play "Teahouse", although written in the guise of an ideologically correct social study of the human landscape of the ancient capital, captures the flavour of old Peking and exudes an ineffable sense of nostalgia for a lost world. Liu Xinwu has actively affected the style of the Peking writer in his fiction even though he is not a native of the city — he was born in Sichuan and still has a distinct "southern" accent. In "The Wish" Liu weaves his fascination with the ambience of the old imperial city into a tale of a couple who weather decades of political vicissitudes. To use the relationship of the worker and the Manchu noblewoman as a central narrative theme in this story was for Liu a marked departure from his earlier work. When "The Wish" was made into a film by Huang Jianzhong in the early 1980s some critics saw it as the beginning of a new style of art cinema in China. "The Wish" has been called, not without justification, a Chinese "On Golden Pond". Liu pursued this theme of nostalgia in some of his other writings and decided to build on his earlier exploration of the Cultural Revolution in a novel he has been working on in recent years.

Liu's achievements as an official writer won recognition in 1986 when he was appointed the editor-in-chief of the prestigious monthly journal *People's Literature*, the chief organ of the Chinese Writers' Association. His incumbency has not been an easy one, however, and shortly after he took over the job, Party General Secretary Hu Yaobang was ousted (January 1987) and a purge of "bourgeois liberalization" was initiated. The first cultural target of the purge was Liu's magazine which was attacked for printing a salacious novel about Tibet. Even in the fairly freewheeling times from late 1987 to mid-1989 Liu has been under many contradictory pressures, political as well as economic. To endure the uncertainties of economic reform has been the lot of all Chinese today, but to suffer from the political fiats of that country's geriatric rulers is something most sorely felt by her writers and intellectuals. Liu has, over the decades, chosen to compete for a place in the entourage of politicians, and the price he has paid for such a privileged position is part of the bargain. While no mean talent, his conscious pursuit of official laurels has meant that he has never gained the stature or confidence of an independent artist. In this he is typical of many of his coevals.

In terms of his art, Liu has had to compete on a relatively open cultural market with younger, more daring writers who have appeared in Peking since the mid-1980s. They include the novelists Xu Xing, Liu Suola and the popular Wang Shuo. Their works, the product of a Chinese punkdom, appeal more directly to their contemporaries in their twenties and thirties, many of whom have over the years formed the basis for China's new urban (petit) bourgeoisie. The political and artistic conventions of the past still hamper writers of Liu's generation in their attempts to compete with the newcomers; burdened by decades of political uncertainty and creative restrictions, they often find themselves at a loss even when given the freedom of expression, or worse, pen works that consciously attempt to be "with it", a futile and somewhat pathetic endeavour.

This volume reflects some of the faces of one of China's most successful middle-aged writers. At times the works contained herein entertain, they often try to educate or elucidate, and more often than not they tell us as much about their author as the unsettled and changing society which he tries to depict.

October 1989
Canberra, Australia

Black Walls

Time: About 7.30 one Sunday morning in summer
Place: A small courtyard in a Peking alley. A few trees are
          growing in the yard; five or six families in residence.

A man by the name of Zhou had a room to himself on the
eastern side of the courtyard. He wasn't a day under thirty, and was
most probably a bachelor, though he used one of those wash basins
with a "double happiness"* design in red on it. Strange that —
maybe he was divorced. Then why did he bow his head bashfully
whenever he met one of the unmarried lasses in the courtyard, and
do his best to avoid them?

Zhou hadn't been living in the courtyard long. He worked in
one of those places with an unpronounceable name. None of the
other residents could figure out what he did for a living. That
didn't really matter; anyway, you could work out his story yourself:

When these stories were written, one *yuan* was worth from 25 to 40 US
cents, ten *fen* from 2.5 to 4 US cents, and one *fen* from .25 to .4 US cents.
* A decorative motif symbolic of marriage.

a man of his age with eight years in the countryside behind him and over seven years of work experience — it wasn't hard to get a pretty clear idea of the type of money he was making and what other perks he enjoyed. All in all it was fairly standard stuff. He hadn't caused any trouble since he'd been living there, nor was he much of a one for dropping in on neighbours. If you bumped into him in the courtyard you might take the initiative by asking, "Eaten yet?" but he'd be sure to reply "Yes, thanks." without a hint of emotion. Or maybe he'd be the first to speak: "Having a rest then?" "That's right, thought I'd sit out here for a spell." Then he'd walk straight on without attempting to stop for a chat.

There were times you'd have a chance of drawing him out a bit, though. In a courtyard like that everyone uses the communal tap for washing clothes, to get drinking water and to rinse the rice for meals. You were always coming across your neighbours at the tap; he'd be there as well. He couldn't very well avoid being sociable on such occasions. But he was no great conversationalist, and even though he'd answer when spoken to, he never asked any questions in return. You couldn't really say the neighbours had warmed to him; but they had nothing against him, either.

Zhou was working up a storm this particular morning. It started when he moved all his things out into the courtyard. Then he set to work mixing some stuff in a large basin. He must have borrowed a spray-gun the day before — one of those gadgets you pump with your foot. It looked as though he was going to repaint his room.

Nothing strange about that. When one of the neighbours went over to the tap he inquired, "You going to paint your room?" "Just a quick spray," he offered in reply. The other man did his best to be neighbourly. "Need a hand?" "No, thanks, I've got a spray-gun. Have it done in no time." And they went about their business happily.

A cicada hidden up in the foliage of the scholar-tree started singing and the song was taken up by its fellows one after the other. Everyone was used to the racket, so no one got annoyed.

About 7.46

"Pshhh — pshhh — pshhh — "

Now that was an unfamiliar sound. It didn't take much guessing to figure out what it was: Zhou had started painting.

Five, no, four to eight

A few of the young people living in the courtyard were going out as it was their day off. They were all dressed up.

One girl who spent her days selling meat had decked herself out in imitation jewelled ear-rings and marched forth in a pair of cream coloured high heels. Her automatic nylon umbrella with a floral pattern in blue burst open the moment she stepped into the street.

The young fellow who worked in a foundry was sporting a jersey he'd got ahold of somewhere with the legend "Indiana University, USA" printed on it. He was wearing a pair of corduroys made for a safari suit — the type of trousers produced for export that had been sold on the domestic market. He put on a pair of tinted sunglasses with extra-large lenses before pushing his fashionable small-wheeled bicycle out the gate.

Then there was the girl who was studying business management at a branch college. She was done up in a pale green skirt that she'd made herself — one that didn't bunch up at the waist. She hurried out carrying a large round straw bag.

What happened then was only possible because they had gone out. But then again it's hard to say whether things would have been any different even if they had stayed at home. That's because one youngster did stay in that day. He sold glassware at a local market and it was his day off too. After breakfast he propped himself up on his bed and lost himself in a novel called *The Unlighted Lamp*. Later, when his mother tried to get him to take part in the morning's drama, he fobbed her off with a scornful laugh and went on reading.

About a quarter past eight

The atmosphere in the courtyard was growing tense, though it would be more correct to say, "the atmosphere indoors" — and in one door in particular. It was the Zhaos' apartment on the northern side of the yard.

Zhao was a man of fifty-six. He'd chosen early retirement so his daughter could take his place in the factory — to "carry on the revolution" as it was called. He'd found temporary employment elsewhere, but when they upgraded the production line at this new place, he was retrenched. Although old Zhao was at a loose end for the moment, he was figuring on landing himself another job soon.

It was only natural that the neighbours had congregated in his place. They'd all come to tell Zhao that young Zhou was painting his walls with black paint, not white. He was going to paint his room black of all things! Now, don't ask what he'd put in the concoction he was using; looked like ink, and it was as dark as pitch.

Apart from the initial shock caused by this sensational news, Zhao felt a deep sense of satisfaction that they'd come to him first. It was ten years ago that he'd been sent to a local performing arts ensemble as an adjunct to a Mao Zedong Thought Workers' Propaganda Team. How well he remembered the conspiratorial glee of the "political activists" who'd come to him to report on the "latest developments in class struggle" amongst their fellow artists.

His wife, who was known to everyone as Auntie Zhao, was lost in a similar reverie. To think it was only eight years since she'd been in charge of this "socialist courtyard". This morning was like old times; in fact, just like the time the neighbours had come to report they'd found the remains of a "reactionary slogan" pasted up on the base of the wall behind the date tree. Memories of events buried in the dead ashes of the past suddenly flickered to life.

"We're not going to put up with that." Zhao took a firm stand from the start.

"What can he be thinking of?" Auntie Zhao chorused angrily.

8.25, or thereabouts. Meanwhile —

"Pshhh — pshhh — pshhh — "

Zhou worked on, unaware of the mounting furore.

News update: HE'S PAINTING HIS CEILING BLACK!

Zhao invited his guests to sit down — it was as though they were going to have a political study meeting. Meetings always leave someone dissatisfied; but this wasn't going to be one of those meetings that bores everyone silly. In fact, it was just the type of meeting that Zhao liked most of all. He took the initiative.

"This calls for immediate action. Let's report him to the police."

Eight or ten years ago this would have been more than enough to set the tone of the proceedings. But things had changed. Weedy Uncle Qian made an objection without a moment's hesitation.

"Listen, I don't think we should be so hasty.... After all, he hasn't done anything illegal."

Old Zhao and his wife stared at him in amazement. You're nothing but an old tailor — they thought in unison. Back in the days when we had you pegged as a petty exploiter you wouldn't have dared talk back like that. Now look at you: just because you make a bit of money by taking in work and sit watching your new colour TV, you think you can speak to us like that?

Damned right he did, sitting there bolt upright on his stool saying exactly what he thought of the matter and at length. He was of the opinion that young Zhou was ailing.... I mean it's been in all the papers: a person gets all excited over something and before long they start doing odd things. Just last week I saw Zhou airing his quilt outside his place — none of you others probably noticed — a quilt, mind you, with its cover made of red satin. Not all that strange, you may say; but wait for it: the underside was bright red as well! You can't tell me that isn't mighty wacky. So I'm saying it's not the police we should be thinking about: what we need is a doctor. Look, there's a retired doctor of Chinese medicine just down the street. Now I'm not sure he's the type of doctor who could cure Zhou of what he's got, but it'd do no harm if we got him to take a look.

There wasn't much of a reaction to Qian's suggestion, for while he was speaking everyone had been gazing out the window. Through the shade of the scholar-tree they could see Zhou working away on his walls blissfully unaware of their concern. He appeared to be singing to himself, and he certainly didn't look sick to them.

The man sitting next to the door scratched his balding pate which was meagrely camouflaged by strands of straggly hair. This was teacher Sun and he had a suggestion of his own to make:

"Well, I think we should go and ask him straight out why he's painting his room black, and if he can't explain himself we'll make him stop — no, persuade him to cease and desist. Yes, that's it, we'll talk him out of it and tell him he shouldn't do it anymore."

Mrs Li, who was conveniently seated at the back of the room, immediately took him up on the idea:

"You're right. You can act as our spokesman."

The others readily agreed.

It was past 8.36

When he had spoken out, Sun naturally assumed that one of the Zhaos would be sent to confront Zhou, so this new development took him completely by surprise. He could have kicked himself for having sat next to the door.

Sun had never taught a class in his thirty years at the primary school. He was in administration. Certainly, he'd been given endless exposure to the finer points of pedantic verbal acrobatics, but now that he had been pushed to the front of the class, he was at a loss as to how he should deal with the situation. He sat facing the others tongue-tied.

8.37

"Pshhh — pshhh — pshhh — " Meanwhile, the painting continued unabated.

The room back on this side of the courtyard was buzzing with a tense and whispered discussion.

Sun was tapping the fingernail of his left thumb mechanically and staring dumbly at the tips of his shoes. He was against confronting Zhou in person. What if he sent him packing? It would be such a loss of face. And how would he explain it to the others? What'd he do if the young brute gave him a browbeating? How would that look? And would he tell the others the truth about it? But that would be tantamount to informing on the man. Should he try and conceal the truth? Yet if he did so, wouldn't he be guilty of deceiving the authorities? On the other hand, there wouldn't be any witnesses, and when they finally got around to reinvestigating the incident nobody would be able to prove anything....

After some moments of soul-searching, which left his brow glistening with large beads of sweat, Sun finally spoke again:

"I still think Old Zhao should be the one to go and ask what he's playing at."

The others immediately followed suit.

"Yes, Zhao, why don't you go and be done with it."

The old worker didn't move a muscle. Finally, when the tenor of public opinion had abandoned casual suggestion in favour of earnest supplication, Zhao jumped to his feet with the words, "Very well, I'll go," after which he stomped out of the room.

He was followed up to the entrance of Zhou's place by the intense gaze of the other residents. They strained themselves in the hope of catching some stray hint of the exchange, but all they could hear was the unbroken staccato of the cicadas.

8.41

Zhao returned to the room ashen-faced only to report:

"The nerve of the man. Says he'll come over and explain when he's finished. I knew he'd try something like this. Do you think he gives a damn about any of his neighbours?"

His wife added to the drama of the moment by pointing out the window and crying furiously:

"Now look what's happened. Here's the man who checks the water gauge. See, he's gawking at Zhou's place. Before you know it people outside will be talking about this, mark my word; and they won't be saying that one oddball decided to paint his walls black. They'll be saying our courtyard is the one with the black walls. We'll be tarred with the same brush."

Mrs Li was employed in a workshop where they teased cotton padding. She was a fairly reasonable character and she now ventured an explanation of Zhou's actions that she hoped would calm everyone down:

"Maybe he's only using the black paint as a base coat, and he's going to paint over it with white anyway."

8.43

"Pshhh — pshhh — pshhh — " The spraying continued and from a distance the room already looked like a black hole. Nobody had taken any notice of her; Mrs Li shot a glance at the other side of the courtyard and her heart sank.

What were you supposed to make of the man? Okay, so he was only painting his place black, but everyone in the courtyard was going to have to live with it. He obviously hadn't given the matter a second thought; but he had no right to implicate innocent bystanders.

8.45

Everyone in the room could agree on one thing: Zhou shouldn't have been painting his room black. How could he do this to them: the walls, the ceiling, everything black? No normal person would have done such a thing. But there he was actually doing it. He was odd, weird, possessed.... It was insane; no, it was downright reactionary....

Zhao still felt that reporting him to the police was the right thing to do. Only he didn't feel quite the same way about the police as he used to, so he was reluctant to go. Ten years or so ago the police station had been converted into the headquarters of the local Steering Committee for Smashing the Reactionary Public Security and Legal Apparatus. At the time, there weren't any real police stations to speak of. The police nowadays lacked the blood-lust of the past, and they were no longer willing to take the initiative. All that nonsense they fed you about "working within official guidelines" — as soon as they gave you that spiel you could be sure they wouldn't take any positive action. In fact, they probably wouldn't do a thing about the black walls. And this is why Zhao hesitated. He still felt an irrepressible urge to make a report, and to do it immediately. It was his responsibility and duty to do so. He wasn't doing this for himself. What could he possibly gain from reporting such a thing?

Auntie Zhao could see her husband was in a quandary and her heart went out to him. How things had changed for them during the past decade. Her old man had fallen on hard times, all because he didn't have a legitimate trade to speak of. He was kept running from pillar to post looking for casual work, taking jobs as a watchman in warehouses, and so on. But none of these jobs lasted very long. It wasn't that he had no trade to call his own in the past, but they kept encouraging him to get involved in political movements. And with all that "moving" back and forth over the last thirty years, he hadn't had the time to acquire a trade. In the present set-up, that meant he had no way of making money. He had been justifiably proud of his political acumen in the past, not that it did him much good now. He was trying to bring his considerable professional talents to bear on the present case, but his eyes, his deeply lined face and his mouth betrayed his many doubts. It was such a pity. Why should he get so worked up about it? It wasn't as though he was going to get anything out of it for himself.

Qian, on the other hand, was more convinced than ever that young Zhou was ill. It was no use getting a doctor of Chinese medicine — Zhou wouldn't let him get close enough to take his pulse. So that was out. They needed a doctor trained in western medicine. But as hospitals never let doctors make house calls anymore, they'd have to convince him to go in for a check-up. That might prove difficult.

Mrs Li felt like going back to her place and dragging that no-good boy of hers away from the book he had his head buried in and get him to think of something. Maybe he could make Zhou stop this silliness. Then they could repaint his place white together.

White was such a lovely colour. How could the walls of a house be anything but white?

Teacher Sun was thinking of slipping off home, but he was too scared to move. He had to be careful to show the right attitude in this matter, so that if the incident was investigated in the future he wouldn't come out looking like a person of confused loyalties. By the same token, when it was Zhou's turn to be vindicated for his actions, Sun didn't want to appear as a man who had taken an active part against him. Ideally he wanted to avoid any form of criticism for any past, present, and future actions. At the moment he felt he'd fulfilled his obligations adequately by his mere presence in Zhao's house, and now it was time to be going. The hard thing was slipping away without raising any eyebrows.

8.48

Zhao had a ten-year-old grandson everyone called Little Button. At first he'd sat through all the fuss with his head lowered over his drawings. After a time he went and sat next to the door leading to the outer room, listening to the discussion intently. To him the room felt cramped and stuffy. He couldn't understand why grown-ups enjoyed being so uncomfortable.

They all started talking again, and just as the discussion was entering a new and heated phase, Little Button walked over to his grandfather, looked up at him and asked:

"Grandad, what are you all talking about?"

"Run along and play. This is grown-ups' talk," Zhao snapped sternly.

But Little Button wasn't deterred.

"I know you're all angry with Uncle Zhou for painting his walls. You don't know him; he's really nice, he's fun to play with. Once he called me into his room and showed me a pile of cardboard pieces. They were as big as the evening paper, and all different colours. He showed them to me one after the other, holding them right up close to my eyes so all I could see was that colour. Then he asked me lots of questions: 'Do you like this one or not? Does it make you feel hot or cold? Wet or dry? Does it smell or not? Does it make you feel like going to sleep or going out to play? What does this one make you think of — or doesn't it make you think of anything? Does this one make you feel scared or not? Does this one make you feel thirsty? Do you want to keep looking at it or not?' He wrote down everything I said in a little book. He's great fun, really. If you don't believe me, just go and see for yourselves."

With this memory still fresh in his mind, Little Button looked up at his grandfather and shouted:

"Grandad, you've been talking for ages now. You must be tired, why don't you let me have a go?"

Everyone in the room suddenly fell silent and looked over at the boy. Zhao waved his hand impatiently.

"All right then, go ahead."

Little Button asked them all:

"Is Uncle Zhou going to come and paint all of our houses when he's finished his?"

8.49

The question left them all speechless for a moment.

8.50

"He wouldn't dare," Zhao spluttered.
"Just let him try," chipped in his wife.
Li and Sun cried in unison, "Certainly not!"

Uncle Qian thought for a moment before responding:

"No, his illness isn't that serious. From what I can tell he'll restrict himself to his own house...."

8.51

Little Button shrugged his shoulders and blinked in amazement. The pupils of his eyes were even darker than Zhou's black walls and they sparkled brilliantly. He laughed innocently and cried:

"There's nothing to worry about then. Uncle Zhou is painting *his* walls, not ours. So why are you all sitting here talking about him?"

8.52

There was complete silence in the room.

"Pshhh — pshhh — pshhh — " The sound of spraying continued to issue from Zhou's room. Accompanied by the song of the cicadas, it was crisp and clear.

Summer 1982
Jingsong Estate, Peking

Bus Aria

Lifeblood of the metropolis.

Anger. When you ride the bus it's hard to avoid. Waiting, bored. Damn bus won't come. When it finally does come, it often zooms right by without stopping, with that little "Express" or "Special" sign propped in the window. Or, you run up to the door and it slams in your face with a bang. Even if you manage to squeeze your way on, the ticket-seller pushes and shoves you from behind, as if you were nothing but a sack of potatoes. If she's feeling energetic, she'll make all kinds of trouble for you when she checks the tickets; if she's not in the mood, she won't trouble herself to sell you a ticket even if you want to buy one.

So many buses parked at the depot. Why don't they dispatch one?

Huddled together, the passengers burn with impatience.

There's a little hut here at the depot; it's the dispatcher's office. A passenger bursts in and shouts: "How come you still don't send out a bus?"

No one pays him any attention.

The dispatcher, who is filling in some forms, pulls a long face. A bunch of young people, all drivers and ticket-sellers, are sitting on a bench absorbed in chit-chat.

The passenger repeats his question, louder.

Several voices answer at once: "Go outside and wait!" "There ain't no buses now!"

Finally a bus pulls up in front of the stop. Jostling one another, the passengers scramble aboard.

Suddenly, the ticket-seller announces: "This bus will not stop at Xidan! If you're going to Xidan, don't get on!"

Xidan is a major downtown stop! Why aren't they stopping there?

Confusion. Some people want to get off and wait for a Xidan bus, but before they can get to the door, the bus has already left the station.

As the bus gets under way, the passengers start to grumble. "Why aren't you stopping at Xidan?" "We're all going to Xidan!" "Even if this is an express, you have to stop at Xidan! Be reasonable!"

The permed and painted ticket-seller up front says sulkily, "Don't grouse at *me*. Talk to the driver."

There is always a certain randomness about which stops an express bus makes; after all, a dispatcher's instructions aren't imperial edicts.

The driver shouts, "First stop, Xidan!"

The ticket-seller takes up the cry: "First stop, Xidan!"

The bus, seventeen metres long and composed of two articulated sections, is packed to the gills with passengers. Some haven't heard this announcement; some haven't heard it clearly; and some aren't even listening.

The dispatcher got accustomed to passengers bursting into the office and shouting questions at her like this a long time ago.

She can't be bothered to answer. It's even too much trouble for her to look up and see who's asking the question.

To the passengers, this tiny dispatcher's office is a world apart.

Hanging on one wall is a big wooden duty board. Each member of the transport team has a little wooden tag with his or her name on it; these are hung on the board according to the work assignments for the day. There is always a group of tags hanging off to one side; these are the absentees.

No wonder all the passengers were so worked up. With so many buses parked around the depot, why don't they send out a few?

During off-peak hours, only half the buses are in use. All the peak-hour drivers have gotten off work and gone home; with no one to drive them, how can the buses go out? Even during peak hours some buses sit around the depot because some drivers don't show up for work.

If the drivers don't show up, there's nothing the dispatcher can do.

She yawns as she fills in her form. One column on the form is for punctuality. She fills the entire column with X's.

If the buses aren't on time, blame the road. Some roads in Peking date back to the Qing dynasty and are only wide enough to accommodate a sedan chair. Or blame the traffic. There are now more than 300,000 motor vehicles and five million bicycles in the city. Blame the traffic lights. Blame the accidents. Blame all kinds of unforeseen delays.

Does anyone understand what the dispatcher's job is like? She works 24 hours at a stretch, and then takes 24 hours off; this is the "day-on, day-off" system. In addition to the dispatcher's office, the transportation team has a block of prefabs. When the last bus returns to the depot, the dispatcher sleeps in one of the rooms there. In bus-driver parlance this is called "crashing at the station".

When they're stuck in traffic, the buses can't make it back to the depot. When they get back at last, they arrive in a clump. Can the dispatcher send them out again like that, stuck together like candied crab apples on a stick? She has to allow a certain distance between them; this is why she sends out specials and expresses. She has her own good reasons for doing what she does, and this is why she pulls a long face when passengers ask questions. If she tells a particular driver not to stop at Xidan, it's because she wants him to get to Dongdan and pick up the big crowd that's amassed at the stop there. Or she might send an empty bus directly to Xidan to pick up the restless passengers waiting there.

She does this sort of thing every day. But the passengers never understand why.

"What's wrong with those dispatchers?" they often say resentfully.

To some degree, this dispatcher is a victim of misunderstanding. She's not making the passengers suffer on purpose. She's a married woman. She has problems with her mother-in-law. Her child is showing symptoms of rickets. Her husband doesn't get along with his supervisor at the factory where he works. She still doesn't own a washing machine. Her checked woollen coat has a big grease spot on it. She's heard there's a new brand of cleaning fluid that works effectively on such spots, but she hasn't been able to find any in the shops yet. She's been dreaming about owning a pair of white leather pumps. Her head itches; she needs a shampoo. She wants to buy a set of Huazi cosmetics. But who cares about all of this?

"What's wrong with you people? Why don't you send out a bus?" Without raising an eyelid, she continues to fill in the form.

The bus stops at Xidan.

A bunch of passengers surge off the bus as if they'd just been relieved of some terrible burden. Another bunch surge on with the feeling that they've gained something rare and precious.

But the bus doesn't budge.

Two young men who have just gotten off push angrily round the front of the bus to the driver's cab. Yanking open the door, one of them yells, "Why the hell didn't you stop at the Labour Union?"

The other stretches out his arm as if he were about to grab the driver, shouting, "You think you know something about driving a bus? Step outside with me!"

The Labour Union was the previous stop. Originally the ticket-seller had announced that the bus would stop there but not at Xidan.

The driver, Han Dongsheng, thought he was doing everyone a favour by stopping at Xidan. He certainly never expected to be ambushed like this.

He is short but solidly built, with thick eyebrows and a heavy beard. From his looks you know he's not to be messed with.

Now it was Han Dongsheng's turn to blow his top. It was only because everyone shouted "Stop at Xidan! Stop at Xidan!" that he let people off there and not at the previous stop. He thinks: If you two wanted to get off at the Labour Union why didn't you say so in the first place? When you try to please people all you get is blame. A while back, when they were repairing the road at Dabeiyao, the traffic jams had often forced the buses to a standstill for half an hour at a time. Anxious passengers would go up to the front and plead: "Driver, please let us off!" According to the rules, the doors can only be opened at bus stops. Han Dongsheng might have ignored these pleas altogether, but being soft-hearted, he would often open the doors for those who wished to get off. This time his heart had softened again. "Let us off at Xidan!" Hearing this chorus of entreaty, his only thought was to make things easier for everybody; he never imagined it would end up causing so much trouble. But look at these two guys going right off the deep end! So they're looking for a fight, eh? He shouts them down, his face turning red: "What d'you think you're doing? Go ahead and hit me. If this bus sits here all day it'll be your fault, not mine."

The two toughs don't touch him; instead, they let fly a stream of abuse.

Han Dongsheng trembles with anger. Turning around, he shouts toward the back of the bus: "Hey! Didn't a whole bunch of you want to get off at Xidan? Remind these guys about it, will ya?"

Only Xia Xiaoli, the ticket-seller working the front of the bus, answers him, "They sure did! They were all howling to get off at Xidan, and now that we're stopped here, a couple of people start bitching."

Not a single passenger says a word.

Han Dongsheng is about to explode. He turns around and starts quarrelling with the two young toughs. He's even ready to hop down off the bus and teach the two of them a lesson.

By this time the traffic at the Xidan bus stop is a hopeless mess. A long string of buses has already pulled up behind this one, and none of them can move. For the moment, the traffic cop at the intersection is too busy to pay attention to this particular bus. Passing pedestrians and cyclists gather round to watch the action.

This is West Chang'an Boulevard, Peking's main thoroughfare. Just ahead is the telegraph office. Little multi-coloured flags are strung across the avenue. The avenue itself is packed solid with cars.

The situation is worsening.

Not a single passenger sticks up for Han Dongsheng.

There's nothing odd about this.

Everybody who was hollering about getting off at Xidan had left the scene long ago. And the passengers who didn't want to get off at Xidan paid no attention to all the shouting about "First stop, Xidan! We're stopping at Xidan!" All they are concerned about is keeping out of any dispute. This attitude is quite common.

Most of the passengers now on the bus boarded at Xidan. They aren't happy with the situation they find themselves in, but they don't really understand how it came about. All they can do is wait patiently.

The traffic cop comes over, as well as a few volunteer cops from a neighbourhood committee.

The two young toughs take to their heels.

Han Dongsheng still refuses to start the bus. Throwing all responsibility to the wind, he shouts at the passengers, "The bus's broken down! Everybody off!"

The traffic cop approaches Han Dongsheng and asks him what's going on.

Furious, Han Dongsheng stares at the spot where the two toughs had been standing and snarls, "If you guys can't catch hoodlums like that, then go ahead and fine me! I've had it for today! I quit!" He fumbles in his pocket for his four Peking Motor Vehicle Traffic Code Infringement Record cards — they're red, yellow, blue, and green — and stuffs them into the cop's hand.

These cards which he carries around in his breast pocket are extremely precious. Most of the time he's scared stiff the cops will take them from him.

The traffic cop remains calm and collected. He gives the cards back to Han Dongsheng, saying, "How about moving this bus out of here?"

Han Dongsheng crosses his arms over his chest, gazes up at the bell tower atop the telegraph office, and says sulkily, "This bus is broken down! It won't budge!"

For the moment, it seems, there's nothing the cop can do to ameliorate the situation, so he goes out and directs the other vehicles out of their jam. The volunteer cops disperse the bystanders. One by one the buses and cars chug away.

Han Dongsheng shouts at the passengers again: "This bus is busted! We ain't going nowhere! Everybody off the bus!"

A dozen or so people do what he says, but most of the passengers don't move, especially those who have seats. It's no easy thing getting a seat on a bus in Peking. Even if these particular seats aren't worth very much anymore, everyone is reluctant to give them up. What's more, the people on the bus are accustomed to waiting. Long experience has taught them that impossibilities can become possibilities if one waits long enough. A few more people climb on through the open door. Xia Xiaoli berates them shrilly: "We're not going anywhere, we're not going! Get off, get off!" But some of them get on anyway. They feel that no matter how things turn out, they can't be totally mistaken if they get on the bus. Who knows when the next bus will show up? Even if this opportunity leads nowhere, at least there's something to show for it right now. It certainly beats an opportunity that hasn't come along yet.

Someone hands money for a ticket to Xia Xiaoli, but she brushes him off impatiently, "No tickets! Where d'you think you're going anyway?"

"But I boarded at the depot," explains the passenger.

"Don't worry about it." Xia Xiaoli is still shaking her head and frowning.

Several taxis cruise by.

Watching the little lit signs on top with TAXI written on them in English, Han Dongsheng feels even more depressed.

He calls those signs "tombstones", and he calls taxi drivers "the guys with the tombstones on top".

He used to admire them. Now he envies them.

Han Dongsheng is thirty-one this year. His father works in a restaurant, making the rice and buns. This is no fancy restaurant, just one of those joints at the head of a lane you hardly notice when you go by. His mother is a housewife. His two younger sisters also work at the restaurant, one cutting the meat and vegetables in the kitchen, the other waiting on tables. His younger brother is the pride of the family: he's got a job laying bricks at one of the universities in the western suburbs. Once, the university distributed reduced-type editions of a famous Chinese dictionary free of charge to all the teachers; and though the administrative staff and manual labourers on campus had no reason to own such an unwieldy brick of paper and ink, the unwritten law guaranteeing the equitable distribution of material benefits to all resulted in Han Dongsheng's brother getting hold of one. He promptly sold it, making forty *yuan* on the deal. At that time Han Dongsheng didn't feel poor compared to his brother, but as this kind of thing began to occur more frequently, his resentment grew. Why were bus drivers only issued two pairs of cotton gloves a year?

Han Dongsheng was among the last bunch of young people in China to be sent down to the countryside to "learn from the peasants". How could he have known that the school-leavers graduating one year after him wouldn't have to go down at all? When working in the fields on the commune, and wiping the sweat off his brow, he would fantasize: How wonderful life would be if I were a worker! Later this dream came true when a small coal mine in Fangshan started recruiting miners. Overjoyed, he went there only to learn the hard way that mining coal is even heavier work than planting fields. He then started fantasizing about going back to the city, and in 1979 got his chance when an old buddy of his father's became team leader of a transportation team in the Peking Bus Company. It was through this "back door" that he returned to the city. Before quitting the mine, however, he had to affix his thumbprint to a statement to the effect that he agreed to being demoted from a grade-four to a grade-two worker. Without a moment's hesitation he smeared his thumb with red ink and made a big, bold impression. At the bus company, he started out with a grade-2 worker's salary. For the first two years, he sold tickets, and then learned how to drive. He found being a driver tolerable for the first two years, but over the course of the last year or so he became increasingly discontented.

This is largely due to the sudden boom in the taxi business.

Peking used to have only a thousand or so taxis, yet one never heard stories of taxi drivers getting rich. Now the city has more than 10,000 of them, and everywhere you hear of drivers rolling in money.

In the entire Peking Municipal Bus and Trolley Company there are only 10,000 drivers. Thus there are now more taxi drivers than bus drivers in Peking.

The taxi business is still expanding rapidly. The largest company, Capital Taxi, owns more than 3,000 cars. The Peking Taxi Company, run by the same company that operates the public buses, has 1,800. Besides these, there are over 100 other taxi companies, with names like Soaring Afar, Peace and Happiness, Sunny-bank, Far East, Peking-Shenzhen, Friendship, Broad Attainment, even Shangri-La — you have to admire their imagination.

In the early 1950s, right after the liberation, pedicab drivers would gaze up at bus drivers and turn green with envy. Now it is the bus drivers who literally look down at the taxi drivers, but it's the former who burn with jealousy.

Han Dongsheng is not even as badly off in this respect as some of his colleagues.

Every day he gets up before dawn.

He lives in a crowded compound in one of Peking's ancient lanes.

His family's single-room home is only ten metres square; the furnishings are very simple. On top of the sideboard, which he made himself, there sits an alarm clock he bought when he got married. The alarm broke two years ago, but he hasn't had it repaired; even without the alarm he's wide awake by 3:30 every morning.

Han Dongsheng, his wife and child sleep in the same bed, which is already out of style — a wooden double. Their son is four. They belong to the Hui nationality, they're Moslems. The Hui Nursery is harder to get into than a major university, and since the Hans don't have any personal connections, they haven't been able to get their son in. This is only one of their many worries. In addition, Han Dongsheng and his wife are still in the bloom of youth, and have strong sexual desires. But now they have to make love in the same bed with a child who is old enough to talk. Any little sound the kid makes, like talking in his sleep or grinding his teeth, is enough to kill their desire and set off bouts of guilt and feelings of inferiority. However, despite problems like this, and some even more serious than this, it is relatively easy for them to maintain their peace of mind. After all, they're hardly worse off than a lot of other couples who live in their compound. One nagging question Han asks himself is: While that guy and I are both drivers, why is he at the wheel of a taxi while I'm still driving a goddamn bus?

While he brushes his teeth and washes his face this question continues to gnaw at him. By 4 a.m. he is out of the lane and on the 203 night-owl route, which takes him to the front entrance of Prospect Hill Park.

Every morning from 3.30 to 4.00, a large number of bus company shuttles congregate at the park gate, where crowds of drivers and ticket-sellers wait to be taken to the dispatching offices of their respective routes. It's a splendid sight — too bad the vast majority of people who ride the buses never get a chance to see it.

On the shuttle, Han Dongsheng chews the fat with his fellow drivers. The most popular topic of conversation is which of their acquaintances have become taxi drivers lately, and how they managed to pull it off, although each new revelation on this topic burns in their hearts like a glowing coal. Han Dongsheng feels it's unjust that most of the guys who get to drive taxis are either the children, relatives or buddies of the higher-ups in the bus company. He has memorized all their names and their family relationships so carefully that if you shook him awake from a deep sleep he could rattle them off verbatim.

While he's preparing for work in the yard or at the depot, he gets even more upset, thinking how the taxis in Peking have become more comfortable and attractive than before. They've got air-conditioning, so they're warm in winter and cool in summer. They've got tape players, so you can listen to the theme song from the Japanese TV show, "Blood Relations", or whatever you please. You can stick an air freshener in the back window, or one of those little toy dogs with a nodding head; you can hang a bunch of plastic grapes from the rear-view mirror, or perhaps a perfume sachet, so your taxi will never be smelly and foul. Moreover, you can refuse a fare whenever you please. And though you're supposed to hand over a certain percentage of your fares in Foreign Exchange Certificates, you can always manage to get hold of some for yourself. Finally, at the end of the day you can drive your taxi home — what a lot of trouble that saves! — and you can use your taxi to run errands for people and make them indebted to you; that's another big advantage.

In the winter, when he's filling the radiator with hot water — especially when he spills it and scalds his hand — Han Dongsheng imagines even more vividly and concretely how wonderful it would be to drive a taxi.

As he's driving through the day, a whole range of thoughts run through his mind. The most difficult one to suppress is: "Why can't I quit and become a taxi driver?"

Salaries for drivers like Han Dongsheng are very low. The average wage of the ten thousand drivers of the Municipal Bus and Trolley Company is only about fifty *yuan* per month. If you drive one of the big articulated buses, you get an extra sixty *fen* per day; add to this the mileage bonus, the petrol conservation bonus and the regular bonus, and by simply showing up for work every day and not having any accidents, you can make about 120 *yuan* a month.

Does Han Dongsheng's family have difficulties making ends meet?

Well, nowadays no one in Peking is starving or freezing to death.

Of course, everyone would like to live a little more comfortably.

In the past, the most common greeting in Peking was, "Have you eaten?"

Food was the most important thing in people's lives.

Nowadays, when friends who haven't seen each other for a while meet, often the first thing they say is, "Have you bought a colour TV yet?"

Black-and-white sets are already out of fashion. No one mentions them anymore.

"Got a colour set yet?"

Moreover, they'll ask, "How many inches is the screen?" And then, "What brand?"

If it's a Peony, Kunlun, Gold Star, Peacock, or any other domestic model, they'll shake their heads and say, "Why didn't you buy a Japanese set?"

If you say it's a Furi, the response will be "Oh, the one made on that imported assembly line. Not bad." If you say Toshiba, National, Sanyo, Sony, Sharp — "Wow! That's great. Made in Japan? How'd you manage that?"

This is the way most people in Peking think these days.

Han Dongsheng and his family find it hard to avoid catching the fever. In addition to this, they have other problems.

Although Han Dongsheng's father-in-law is not very old, he's been partially paralysed for more than ten years.

Han's wife, Qin Shuhui[1], explained the entire situation to him

---

[1] In China today few women take their husband's surname, though children usually adopt their father's surname.

during their courtship.

His father-in-law's paralysis makes it very difficult for him to get about, and he has a rather prickly temper.

The old man lives in a small, dark room next to theirs. He keeps a trunk by his bed that is so old it is impossible to determine its original colour. It's supposedly made of camphorwood, but Han Dongsheng has never noticed that it gave off any scent. Nobody is allowed to disturb that trunk; if little Jingjing so much as touches it, his grandfather will warn him away, his mouth twitching at the corners.

Many curious stories about the old man circulate among the older residents in the courtyard. They all know he's a retired grade-seven worker, partially paralysed, well over the hill. But the story goes that about thirty years ago he was something of a playboy, and an accomplished amateur singer of Peking opera. He could perform the arias from "White Gate Mansion" as well as the famous Ye Shenglan. He had his days of glory; he has his secrets, too. One might be able to piece together his life history, but no one will ever penetrate the private history of his heart. Now all the sweetness and mysteries of his youth are packed away in that trunk. Rumour has it that the trunk contains programmes from all the Peking operas staged during the 1930s and 1940s, a big stack of old Peking opera magazines, and a collection of photographs of him posing with such leading opera stars as Mei Lanfang, Xiao Cuihua, Xun Huisheng, Yan Huizhu and Liang Xiaoluan, as well as as some lesser lights, in and out of costume, all of them autographed.... Come the Cultural Revolution, with its movement to smash the Four Olds, he was already a very ordinary worker; no Red Guards raided his house. Now those mementoes in his big trunk are valuable cultural relics. If the scholars at the Chinese Theatre Research Institute ever found out about his collection, they would surely take the necessary steps to acquire it, but it is highly unlikely the old man's story will ever pass beyond the confines of their small lane. When Han Dongsheng heard this story for the first time, he just smiled. He was even a bit disappointed — he had hoped the trunk contained gold ingots or silver bars, or at least a few pieces of jewellery.

Han Dongsheng doesn't know the first thing about Peking opera; in fact, he doesn't like any form of traditional Chinese theatre.

He doesn't read much, either. In fact, you won't find a single book, magazine or newspaper in their home.

He may have a foggy notion of who Mei Lanfang is. But he is more familiar with the names of pop singers like Momoe Yamaguchi and Cheng Lin, and certainly admires them a great deal more.

Han Dongsheng didn't make a fuss about Qin Shuhui's family situation. Shuhui's mother died many years ago, leaving only her father in the condition described above. Yet Han Dongsheng went ahead and married her. It's not easy for Hui people to find suitable spouses. If the shoe fits, wear it.

Since Qin Shuhui's family's quarters were somewhat more spacious than his own family's, he decided to move in with them. Things haven't gone too badly for them.

From the time Jingjing was born, Qin Shuhui hasn't put in a single day at the sweater factory where she worked. She's stayed home on "sick leave", collecting thirty *yuan* a month. This is hardly enough to live on, but what else can she do? She can't get the child into a nursery, and there's her disabled father to take care of. He used to be able to make himself a bowl of instant noodles, but now he can barely hold a bowl level. More serious is the fact that lately the old man's been suffering from incontinence, so now she has to wash both his and Jingjing's underwear. Just imagine! She's considered hiring an amah, but she's never been able to figure out how they could afford it. Better to stay at home and continue her "sick leave". "I'm self-employed," she consoles herself.

Once when driving along Ritan Road, Han Dongsheng suddenly screeched the bus to a halt, jumped out, grabbed a careless cyclist by the arm and gave him a bawling-out. On the face of it Han scolded the cyclist because the fellow had broken the traffic rules and gotten in the bus's way; actually, though, this all came about because Han Dongsheng had been holding back his anger since the previous afternoon, and was waiting for an opportunity to let it loose on someone. Earlier that afternoon, Shuhui had taken their son Jingjing shopping. While they were gone, the old man lost control of his bowels, and lay there puffing and gasping in a suffocating fetor. Han Dongsheng could hardly stand by and not help him; he cleaned up the mess, but the whole incident repulsed him. He thought to himself: On the road I take care of passengers all day, and at home I have to nurse a sick old man. But we don't even have a colour TV yet! What's the matter with me?

Sometimes an ugly thought rears up in Han Dongsheng's mind: It's about time the old guy... But he can always suppress this thought with a little effort.

When the old man is feeling a little better, he manages to speak, although it sounds more like gargling. He'll call to Han Dongsheng:

"Buy me a couple of packs of cigarettes!"

With trembling hands, Han Dongsheng's father-in-law gives him a one *yuan* note. Han accepts it silently. The old man has a reasonably generous pension, but he doesn't give all of it to the couple; he only contributes 15 *yuan* a month for food, and keeps the rest for himself. He's a heavy smoker and tea-drinker, so when he runs out of these items, he asks Han and his wife to buy more for him. When he's feeling his healthiest, he may even totter out to take a bit of sun and bring Jingjing back a few treats. These are the dimensions of their financial relationship.

Han Dongsheng comes back with the old man's cigarettes: one pack of Jade, forty-four *fen*; one pack of Plum Blossoms, forty-seven *fen*. These are the only two brands his father-in-law smokes. Han Dongsheng hands over the cigarettes and the nine *fen* in change, and the old man accepts them with his quivering fingers.

Watching his father-in-law's twitching face, Han Dongsheng feels a surge of pity. A thought wells up from his heart: "We all have to grow old sometime...."

The ability to put oneself in another's place is one of the finest human qualities.

There's nothing more inaccessible than the human heart. It's extremely difficult to empathize with others.

But the desire to do so is a vital human attribute.

There's nothing easy about it.

It's hard to nurture this desire in everyone.

Life is a net.

The passengers on a bus are like a school of fish swimming from one knot in the net to another. Their time on the bus may be spent lost in numbed reverie or self-absorption. To them, "bus driver" and "ticket-seller" are abstract concepts; even though the living, breathing ticket-seller is sitting before them, they remain oblivious to the fact that she has a name, her own history, her own life to lead, a family of her own, and that she experiences anger, grief and joy....

Of course, one can't blame the passengers for this.

When they suffer indignities at the hands of the drivers and ticket-sellers, they are innocent.

The passengers that Han Dongsheng yelled at to get off the bus at Xidan were all victims of his stubbornness and wrath.

Nobody has it easy on the bus.

A few of the passengers Xia Xiaoli and Han Dongsheng yelled at were actually deeply hurt by what they said.

One of them is the man who tried to buy a ticket but was rudely rebuked by Xia Xiaoli. He is a cadre who works as a technician in a state-run factory.

Han Dongsheng feels wronged because he makes less money than a taxi driver, but this cadre makes even less than he does.

In terms of basic salary alone, this forty-year-old cadre earns more than Han Dongsheng. But Han and his co-workers receive bonuses and supplements that push up their monthly income to 120 or 130 *yuan*, while the balding cadre gets a flat salary plus a bonus that add up to a little more than 100 *yuan* a month.

Some of Han Dongsheng's colleagues have a second source of income.

Often they will call in sick, although in fact they are in perfectly good health. They've gone to Guangzhou or some other city to pick up a vehicle for a company. By driving day and night they can make it back to Peking within a week or two; one such trip can earn them as much as 600 *yuan*.

Han Dongsheng lacks the courage to do this sort of thing. Even if he were brave enough, Qin Shuhui would not let him.

Two years ago, their neighbourhood committee arranged a job for Qin Shuhui, assembling paper boxes at home, the fancy kind used to pack Western-style suits. For pasting together a big box, she could earn 3.6 *fen*; for a small one, 2.4 *fen*. Since Han Dongsheng worked the morning shift, he was out of the house before sunrise, and got home at 1:30 in the afternoon. After lunch and a short nap, he and Qin Shuhui would assemble boxes together.

They would work straight through to dinner, and continue after dinner while watching television. At 9.00 Han Dongsheng would go to bed, while Qin Shuhui would keep working until 11.00 if she had the energy.

On their best days they could assemble about 200 boxes.

When they turned in the boxes at the end of the month, they would collect about eighty *yuan*; this was after deducting small amounts for glue, spoilage and a ten per cent commission to the neighbourhood committee.

The cadre we were speaking of, who usually rides his bike to work and only takes the bus occasionally, has no second source of income. Neither he nor his wife, who is also a cadre in a state-run enterprise, dare to try anything like that, nor do they have any opportunity to do so. People say that when cadres are assigned housing they get better flats. This isn't necessarily so, although in general they do better than bus drivers and ticket-sellers. In fact, this cadre was recently assigned a two-bedroom apartment, and though Han Dongsheng and his buddies might not believe it, it is miserably furnished. The cadre and his wife would like to buy a few new electrical appliances; they've been watching the same old 12-inch black-and-white TV for years. Since they've got a TV, they'll leave off thinking about a colour set for a while so they can save up for the washing machine they so urgently need. If they want a two-tub model, it will take them even longer.

In addition to a Kunlun brand 14-inch black-and-white TV, Han Dongsheng's family has a Weili brand combination washer-spinner made in Zhongshan county, Guangdong. Qin Shuhui bought two metres of patterned velveteen to make a dust-cover for it, one way of demonstrating that it occupies the place of honour in their household.

Han Dongsheng has no right to feel sorry for himself, to feel that he is an underdog; but these are the very feelings that caused him to cast aside his responsibility to his work and his passengers as a result of that little incident at Xidan.

If the passengers only knew something about his life at home!

Buying that washing machine was no small matter for them. The money for it came from their own hard labour, pasting boxes together. Who could have foreseen that after using it twice it would break down?

Furious, Han Dongsheng had borrowed a flatbed tricycle, pedalled the washing machine back to the store, and demanded a replacement.

The clerk at the store told him to leave the machine in their warehouse for a while; they would have to examine it to determine whether the machine itself was defective or if the owner had failed to operate it according to the instructions. Han Dongsheng got impatient and quarrelled with him. But such arguing was futile, just as futile as when the passengers on the bus argue with him. The power to make a decision — no matter how insignificant it was — was in the other guy's hands.

So he left the machine there. The next day on the bus, Han Dongsheng was so upset that on several occasions he slammed on the brakes so hard that many of the passengers lost their footing. Not a single passenger knew that apart from sheer physical inertia, the other factor behind these jolts was the emotional state of the driver. They were even less aware that this had anything to do with a particular washing machine sitting in a department store warehouse.

To make a long story short, after two more trips to the store, Han Dongsheng and Qin Shuhui finally got back the machine that is now sitting proudly beneath its velveteen cover. This one is a real beauty — not a single bug in it.

But the minor joys and sorrows in their lives keep rolling in like waves breaking on the shore.

One day Han Dongsheng returned home from work and found Qin Shuhui sitting on the bed crying.

What had happened?

Someone had laid a maggot on them, informing the

neighbourhood committee that Qin Shuhui already had a regular income. Henceforth they would no longer be able to assemble boxes.

Han Dongsheng was jealous of taxi drivers. He had never imagined that anyone could possibly be jealous of *him*.

He was enraged. Did those snitchers think it was easy earning that extra eighty *yuan* a month? At times, in order to meet a deadline, he worked with his wife until midnight. The next morning he would almost fall asleep at the wheel. What if he had an accident and had his licence revoked, or went to jail? Wouldn't his wife and child starve?

Han Dongsheng thought angrily: Are we supposed to split that eighty *yuan* with those snitchers, or what? Is that what they want?

Actually, Han Dongsheng should have asked: Do taxi drivers have it that easy? They might make a lot of money, but they work longer hours than bus drivers, sometimes sixteen or eighteen hours a day, never less than twelve. You call that easy? Should they split the extra money they make with all the bus drivers in Peking? Is that right?

Red-eyes: a disease caused by envy. It's probably the most common mental disease in China today.

After Han Dongsheng and Qin Shuhui lost the job assembling boxes, they sought another path to riches. Qin Shuhui made friends with somebody in the post office,[2] and they began to sell newspapers.

For selling one copy of the *Peking Evening News* they could earn 0.4 *fen* profit. Copies of *Wide World* and *Sports Fan* yielded an average of 0.5 *fen* each. Every day, they buy 300 copies of the *Peking Evening News* and 200 copies of *Wide World* and *Sports Fan*. Penny by

---

[2] In China magazines and newspapers are distributed by the post office.

penny they pile up their fortune.

Each day after work, Han Dongsheng goes out on the street and sells newspapers; he can make a little more than two *yuan* per day. Each day, when Qin Shuhui counts the day's earnings — all of it in coins and wrinkled paper currency in small denominations — she says with satisfaction, "We've made enough for a day's food!"

China is famous the world over for its cuisine.

But the daily meals of the vast majority of Chinese are simple in the extreme.

Most ordinary Peking residents prefer to spend as little as possible on food and save their money for major appliances.

Nowadays the best way to tell whether a Peking family is well off is not to look at the way they eat or dress or even at the furniture and decorations in their home, but rather to take stock of the number and quality of electrical appliances and high-class consumer goods they own.

In China there's something called the "eight major purchases". The first place is invariably occupied by the colour TV. The other seven items are ranked by each person according to his own preference: refrigerator, washing machine, sewing machine, tape recorder, camera, motor-scooter and video cassette player.

In order to expedite their acquisition of the "big eight", Han Dongsheng and family economize on food. Every morning he goes to work without breakfast. After driving for a few hours, he stops at a little Muslim snack shop near the depot and buys four deep- fried crullers which he washes down with a little tea. He eats the same thing every day. At noon, he goes home for lunch. Everyone in the compound knows what's on the menu. 365 days a year, it's noodles with a dollop of fried bean paste. Qin Shuhui fries a new batch of this paste every three days. Although she is reasonably generous with the oil, she only adds a few eggs and a few dried shrimp shells, but never any ground mutton. Since the price of mutton rose to 3.80 *yuan* per kilo, they only buy it once a month, and even then only 500 grammes at a time. In the evening they eat boiled rice with a few stir-fried dishes. Qin Shuhui buys the cheapest vegetable on the market. Lately green peppers have been quite affordable, thirty-two *fen* per kilo, so she has been frying up an entire kilo of them every day.

That cadre who was refused a ticket has no way of knowing that the driver of the stranded bus lives like this.

Xia Xiaoli's response makes him embarrassed and angry.

The cadre says testily, "Why won't you sell it to me? This is a public bus, so I've got to buy a ticket. I refuse to cheat the State!" Stubbornly he holds out a ten-fen note.

Xia Xiaoli pushes his hand away impatiently, tips back her head, narrows her eyes, and juts out her chin. Speaking rapid-fire, as if spitting out grapeskins, she says, "Oh, get away from me!"

Not only does she refuse to sell the cadre a ticket, she even refuses to acknowledge the reasonableness of his argument. It's difficult for the other passengers to keep silent.

One white-haired woman says, "Hey, it's you who are in the wrong...."

Xia Xiaoli cuts her off sharply: "I'm wrong, I'm wrong, I'm wrong...what of it?"

Her haughty eyes bulge like a pair of pea-pods.

A scholarly-looking type wearing glasses, speaking with a bit of a stutter, bursts out with: "Wh-wh-what — what kind of attitude is that? Ha-ha-how can you act this way?"

"That's my attitude! Take it or leave it! I'm quitting!"

Her tone is resolute.

How true the saying, "Before one wave recedes, another breaks." Now the situation on the bus is even tenser than before. Pity the poor passengers!

Xia Xiaoli graduated from a middle school in the outskirts of Peking, where she lived with her parents, both of them factory workers. Her school was an ordinary one; in her entire graduating class only three students made it into university. At the time of her graduation, the Peking Public Transport Company was advertising jobs for ticket-sellers. She answered the ad on her own initiative.

Who could have predicted that after the new economic policies were instituted in China, the "individual enterprise sector" of the economy would develop so rapidly? You never hear about enterprises that go bankrupt or barely scrape by; you only hear tales of how so-and-so has made a bundle. And they aren't all exaggerations. One of Xia Xiaoli's classmates is now the Candied Crab Apple King in the area around her school. With the candied crab apples on a stick he makes at home he's cornered the wholesale market in his neighbourhood. No one knows how much he's put away in the bank, but it is plain to see that he already owns the "big eight". In fact, he has even invited Xia Xiaoli to his house to watch videos. Comparing her situation with his, Xia Xiaoli feels increasing regret over her dumb insistence on taking the ticket-seller's job. If she'd known things would turn out this way, she would have stayed at home for a while, waiting for a chance to get a business permit and start an enterprise of her own. After all, she's no dummy.

Xia Xiaoli never used to pay much attention to her clothes. But of late a whole host of fashionable things have begun to tempt her. Just when she thought the Huazi line of cosmetics was the latest word, the television started advertising Wella Balsam. Soon after she bought an eyebrow pencil, the cosmetics counter at the department store started selling eyebrow tweezers as well. Lately Hong-kong-style beauty parlours have been popping up all over Peking, staffed exclusively by skilled beauticians from Guangzhou. "Little Paris", "Autumn Girl", "New Wave", "Mini" — the names of these places alone are enough to make a young woman's heart go pitter-patter. Having been to a few fashion shows, she knows what the "international colour of the year" is, and has mastered such terms as X-shape, H-shape and A-shape. The Lido Department Store on the elevated mall on East Chang'an Boulevard stocks so many kinds of jewellery, both real and paste.... But when she bought a pair of high-heeled pumps, someone told her that no one was wearing heels this year.

The passengers should really try to understand Xia Xiaoli's feelings and be patient with her.

She's no dazzling beauty, but she is in the prime of youth. Besides, her love of beauty is a commendable trait, nothing to be scorned.

The problem is that she is increasingly dissatisfied with her job. She hates wearing the blue company uniform and its yellow buttons with the steering-wheel design. The cloth is so cheap. The transportation team leader claims that each outfit is worth forty-eight *yuan*, but when Xia Xiaoli took it to a second-hand shop to get an estimate on it, they only offered her nine *yuan*. She refuses to obey the regulations and wear the uniform. On the job, she dresses as she pleases.

She is jealous of female passengers who dress better than herself, especially those who come from out of town.

Once a woman from a remote province asked her, "Comrade, where do I change for the Summer Palace?"

Looking at her out of the corner of her eye, Xia Xiaoli noted her tailored Western-style suit and the flashes of light from her earrings; were they pure gold or just electroplate? "What a get-up!" she thought to herself. It's obviously her first time in Peking — listen to her timid little whine — and she doesn't even know where the Summer Palace is! Xiaoli sneered and said arrogantly, "This bus doesn't go to the Summer Palace! If you want to change buses, get off and ask somebody!"

Naturally the woman's feelings were hurt. It was her first time in Peking, and she had thrilled as they passed by Tiananmen Square moments before. This was the capital. She had expected everything and everyone here to be a notch above everywhere else in the country. She was ecstatic at the prospect of taking a stroll in the Summer Palace. People at home were waiting to hear all the details of what she saw in the capital. But even a simple question about how to change buses had brought a chilling response from this Peking ticket-seller, whose eyes reminded her of moth-balls.

She could not keep from speaking her mind: "Comrade, how can you talk like that?"

"Talk like what?" Xia Xiaoli shot back. "I'm talking Peking dialect. Understand? I told you this bus ain't going to the Summer Palace; what are you going to do about it?"

The woman was getting agitated: "What kind of attitude is that?"

"Like it or lump it!" Xia Xiaoli said with a toss of her head. "Try taking a taxi! Or how about a limousine?"

The woman in fancy clothes fought back tears of rage. All her excitement about the Summer Palace evaporated into thin air.

Often passengers think: Why doesn't the bus company take stern measures against employees like Xia Xiaoli? If they don't change their ways, why not just fire them?

Such suggestions have actually been offered to the bus company in letters and over the phone. There's nothing strange or unreasonable about these suggestions. Weren't the television and the movies full of "tales of the economic reforms" a couple of years ago? Newly appointed "reformists" with "iron fists" were giving slackers and troublemakers the old "fried squid treatment":[3] You

---

[3] A Southern Chinese expression which means giving someone the sack.

won't get down to work? You won't change your ways? You're still making trouble? OK then, scram!

But Xia Xiaoli and her colleagues are hardly intimidated by such measures; actually they welcome them with open arms.

A full twenty-five per cent of the ten thousand bus drivers in the city have requested transfers to other work units. Some even want to quit outright. Others have gone looking for new sources of income without even waiting for approval — they simply don't show up at work.

There are a few ticket-sellers who are doing this kind of thing, too. Xia Xiaoli herself even applied to be let off once. When her application was turned down, she took her anger out on the passengers. Often she doesn't bother to sell tickets. Company regulations stipulate that bonuses will be paid even if ticket sales don't reach the quota. If ticket sales exceed this quota, however, there is an additional bonus, but it's negligible. Most passengers on Xia Xiaoli's route have monthly passes; hardly anyone buys tickets. At any rate, since she knows she won't get that extra bonus, she makes no effort at all to sell tickets.

Xia Xiaoli is not afraid of getting fired; at one point, she even "quit".

A few months ago, she suddenly stop showing up at work. When her transportation team supervisor went to her home, Xiaoli's parents told him, "Who knows where she went. Maybe to Shenyang to see her aunt." Actually she never left Peking. With the help of that Candied Crab Apple King she had gotten in touch with a foreign trade firm and started working as a receptionist, which mostly involved serving tea to foreign businessmen. Even though it was a "temporary job", and the salary was no better than what she earned as a ticket-seller, the job had a few attractive perks, and Xia Xiaoli felt it was at once respectable and undemanding.

However, the transportation team eventually caught up with her and explained the true story to her new employers, who of course had to let her go.

Finally Xia Xiaoli returned to the dispatcher's office wearing the nifty uniform she had got at her temporary job, a smart Hongkong-style sky-blue necklace, snowflake earrings and stylish light-blue vinyl pumps.

It was a case of a "newly appointed official returning in glory to his native village"!

When he walked into the dispatcher's office and saw her for the first time in weeks, Han Dongsheng had no feeling whatsoever that she had done anything wrong. He merely exclaimed jokingly, "So! You traded in your Volkswagen for a Mercedes."

The female ticket-sellers crowded around Xia Xiaoli, some feeling the material of her suit, some asking where she had had her hair done and how much it had cost, some wrinkling their noses and sniffing her perfume. Extremely pleased, Xia Xiaoli stood complacently on one foot, while a colleague tried on one of her shoes. This girl blushed deeply and felt a strange surge of emotion as she put it on.

"Hey!" Xia Xiaoli called to Han Dongsheng, "Have some preserved prunes!"

She'd brought a package of these and laid them on the dispatcher's table, inviting everyone to try them.

Han Dongsheng took one.

"They serve these to foreign businessmen now, not that cheap toffee anymore," she said, displaying her mastery of the mysterious ways of foreign trade.

The dispatcher ate one. Chewing it, she asked Xia Xiaoli, "So, when are you coming back to work?"

As if bestowing a favour upon her, Xia Xiaoli answered, "How about tomorrow?"

Disciplinary action? Firing? From company heads to team leaders, all the managers know such drastic measures are not as effective as constantly reminding the drivers and ticket-sellers that they are lifetime employees of the company. As over a third of the drivers and ticket-sellers have requested transfers due to inadequate salaries, it has been very difficult for the company to maintain a good attendance rate. The most management can hope for is to keep its employees from running off and finding other jobs; if they try this, the company can use the same strategy that it used with Xia Xiaoli. If the bus company doesn't release them, they won't be able to get an individual entrepreneur's permit or find permanent work in another unit. Once discovered, as in Xia Xiaoli's case, the only thing they can do is submit to their fate and go back to driving buses and selling tickets.

Lifeblood of the city.

Poor circulation.

High cholesterol? Blood clots? Varicose veins?

Oh China! Oh Peking! You're struggling forward.

Too many people. Too many crowds. But there is still no tri-level public transportation system to ease the press of the most concentrated moving stream of humanity on earth.

The public transport systems in major cities abroad operate on at least three levels. The lowest is the subway train, the highest is the elevated rail system; and at ground level are the buses and trolley-buses.

The most heavily utilized of these is the subway.

For instance, in Paris, the web-like Metro has over 190 kilometres of track and more than 370 stations. The average number of passenger journeys per day is four million, which makes it far and away the most important form of public transport in that city.

Peking has only two subway lines, not yet connected to each other,[4] comprising altogether only 39.5 kilometres of track with twenty-nine stations. The annual total of passenger journeys on public transport in Peking adds up to more than 3,000 million (or eight million per day), but the subway only accounts for about 100 million or so, or 3.2 per cent of the annual passenger load.

Peking has no elevated railway, so naturally the burden of public transport falls almost entirely on the buses and trolley-buses. There are currently 158 bus and trolley-bus routes in the city, covering a total distance of 1,886 kilometres. A total of 4,009 coaches carry about 8.56 million passengers a day. By contrast, Paris in 1980 had 219 bus and trolley-bus routes covering 2,339.9 kilometres; 3,992 coaches carried a mere 2.08 million passengers a day. The planned capacity of Peking buses and trolley-buses is nine passengers per square metre; in fact, during rush hour the buses carry about thirteen passengers per square metre. The capacity of Paris buses is set at six passengers per square metre, but since they operate at only seventy per cent capacity, usually there are only three or four passengers per square metre. No wonder Peking buses are stuffed to overflowing, while on Parisian buses few people ever have to stand!

But — no matter how good Paris transport is, it's still in France!

You may gaze hungrily at the fish in the pond, but you'd do better to make your own net!

Quite a few people are working on that net.

The cadres of the Peking Public Transport Company are naturally eager to make their enterprise strong and vital and to raise the quality of service throughout the system.

The company has even established a research institute for

---

[4] The two lines were connected in 1987.

urban transport, which is housed in a cramped old leaky building. The forty or fifty researchers there make even less than Han Dongsheng, and spend their time diligently studying statistics and compiling reports.

The members of the Urban Management Committee of the Peking Municipal Government are also doing all they can to solve the complex problems of the capital's public transport system. Some of the leading cadres are literally losing sleep over this vexatious task. It's easy to accuse them of bureaucratism, but just try doing their job — could you reform the entire Peking transport system? It's not easy.

We won't discuss the more concrete difficulties here. It's hard enough just to define the basic role of China's urban public transport.

Should public transportation systems be self-sufficient enterprises responsible for their own profits and losses? Or should they be fully subsidized by the government as utilities serving society at large?

So far, the government has not made up its mind. Public transport is temporarily labelled a "service-oriented production department".

But herein lies an insuperable contradiction.

Since public transport is service-oriented, profit must not be put ahead of everything else; in fact, certain losses must be tolerated. At present, each new bus route in Peking means the loss of a certain amount of money; some routes never earn any money. If the goal is providing service, you can't raise fares. However, the cost of petrol keeps increasing, and the municipal finance bureau continues to tax it. The central government now provides a subsidy of 1.9 *yuan* for every monthly bus pass sold. Although this brings in roughly 32 million *yuan* a year, it barely stems the tide of red ink. Actually, it's only a way for the company to recoup a small percentage of their capital. Under these conditions, company cadres cannot hope for higher wages, and of course drivers and ticket-sellers cannot get higher wages either. And fringe benefits can only be maintained at a very low level.

But since public transport has also been designated as a "production department", everyone in the system is out to increase profits, which has given rise to widespread money grubbing. This means stuffing the buses with passengers to the absolute limit. Transport systems in some Chinese cities have already been thrown into chaos. As "production units" responsible for their own profits and losses, they divert buses to the tourist trade, leaving the bare minimum on regular routes. Also, in order to earn extra cash, some ticket-sellers overcharge passengers and pocket the difference, or collect money without handing out tickets; drivers stop at fewer stops in order to complete more rounds each day, or refuse to leave the depot until the buses are packed to the gills; drivers and ticket-sellers are nasty to the passengers and stage slow-downs because they earn less than the crews carting tourists about.... Peking's public transport system is certainly better than most in China — at least it has never experienced internal chaos of this sort. But since the drivers and ticket-sellers are not making as much money as they would like, moonlighting is prevalent.

In the early morning of 21 August 1985, a female driver on Route 44 who had been at work for less than three hours — when her concentration should have been at its peak — ran her bus smack into a group of people waiting for another bus at Maweigou. A middle-aged woman engineer, who had both her parents and children to support, died instantly; a young man who was just about to start university lost an eye; and two other innocent bystanders were seriously injured. This driver was in fact a kind-hearted woman, with a good driving record; how had this disaster come about? She fell asleep at the wheel — in the middle of the morning! How come? The reason should be obvious.

What *should* a public transport system be?

Most Western capitalist countries have a clearly stated policy on public transport: city buses and trolley-buses are instruments of social benefit; they are not expected to show a profit, and are often not held responsible for losses. A regular policy of financial subsidization is employed. For instance, only thirty-six per cent of the revenue of urban transport in France comes from the fare box: the remaining sixty-four per cent is provided by the national and local governments and organizations which are beneficiaries of the system. In this way the transport company can recover all of its capital, and reinvest money in improvements. This also enables bus drivers to earn fairly high salaries and good fringe benefits. Bus drivers in Paris, for example, earn about 6,000 francs a month, about the same as a French taxi driver.

To cite the example of another socialist country, Hungary, like China, used to have no clear policy on public transport. Financial losses were serious, and drivers were not enthusiastic about their work. In the late 1970s, the Hungarian government adopted policies designed to revitalize the food, entertainment and service industries. While making these industries self-supporting, the government made an exception for public transport, freeing it from financial obligations and placing it in the public utilities sector. In the early 1980s the Hungarian government spent an enormous sum on a complete overhaul of the public transport system in Budapest. Fares remained low, but the level of subsidization was greatly increased, until fares accounted for only twenty-five per cent of the system's total revenue, the government providing the remaining seventy-five per cent. This has brought the income of drivers to a level that actually makes the job appealing.

When public transport, like the postal service, the customs and other government services, no longer needs to compete with other enterprises and enjoys solid financial backing from the government, public transport workers will naturally take pride in their work and be satisfied with their income; this will in turn raise the quality of service.

Well, then, let's subsidize public transport! The more the better.

Of course public transport is not the only sector that needs to be subsidized in China. Basic education — kindergartens, primary schools, middle schools — needs more money too. When you see primary and middle schools turned into guesthouses on holidays and the teachers eagerly attending to the needs of tourists in an effort to improve their straitened circumstances, it's enough to give you a lump in your throat. And don't public cultural institutions deserve more? Library reading rooms are being turned into commercial video parlours showing the worst sort of Taiwan- and Hongkong-made kung-fu films; in our museums you have to buy a ticket for each separate exhibition, and major historical sites are being rented out to film and television studios, as well as to pedlars and merchants, resulting in damage to cultural relics and the pollution of the environment. Isn't this something to get angry about? There are simply too many organizations to subsidize, and too many examples of proper measures taken in other countries: the educational facilities in primary and middle schools in the West are first-rate; schoolchildren enter museums free; shops are not allowed to operate in scenic spots, and in some places no cars are allowed....

But subsidies require enormous sums of money.

Where is this money to come from?

Experience has shown that the restrictive economic policies of the past were inefficient and slow to produce profits, thus making it difficult for China to grow prosperous, and forcing on everyone an equal share of thin rice gruel dished out from the common pot. Experience has also shown that only by adopting policies to stimu-

late the domestic economy and open China to the outside world
can we liberate the nation's productive forces and improve the
people's livelihood.

But economic progress brings with it inequalities.

Some organizations, some people, enjoy the benefits first.

Other organizations and people get them a bit later.

Still other organizations and people, such as the public transportation system and its drivers and ticket-sellers, find themselves
disadvantaged when compared with taxi drivers and independent
entrepreneurs.

Because we're poor, we must institute reforms. Yet this means
widening the gap between rich and poor. Eliminating that gap
means going back to the big pot of gruel. If we don't want to live
drab, impoverished lives we must adopt these policies, but this
means tolerating differences in income. This is a truly difficult
proposition, a vicious circle.

Hamlet ponders: To be, or not to be: that is the question.

Countless Chinese are saying: "To reform, or not to reform: that
is the question."

Let us return to the bus at Xidan.

The situation has reached an impasse.

Some passengers have gotten off, but since no buses have come
to pick them up, some of them stand around the stop resentfully
while others get back on the bus.

Han Dongsheng is still on strike. Xia Xiaoli is shouting at the
passengers at the top of her voice: "It's broken down, it's broken
down, it's broken down, this bus is out of service, kaput! We're not
going nowhere, get off everybody, get off!"

Some of the passengers try to talk reason with her.

"There's nothing wrong with this bus. Why are we still standing
here?"

"What do you think you're doing? What gives you the right not to drive if you don't feel like it?

"Let's get going! We're blocking traffic!"

The argument is intensifying on both sides.

"Even if it's not broken down we're not going anywhere, we're not moving!"

"What the hell is going on here? Such nerve! I'm going to see to it that your superiors find out about this!"

"That's fine with me! Go ahead and do it! Ring up the company: 337036, extension 366; get off the bus and call them!"

"You have no right to treat passengers this way!"

"Then write a letter to the complaint column of the *Peking Evening News*! Get it written up in the papers!"

After a while, the arguments on both sides become somewhat unreasonable.

The attitudes of both passengers and bus employees are, frankly speaking, a bit "reactionary".

Neither side is satisfied with the way things are.

Some of the passengers think: What is the world coming to? Everything's going downhill.

Han Dongsheng and Xia Xiaoli think: "What kind of a life is this? I've had it!"

The ability to inflate small incidents out of all reasonable proportion, and to express themselves in vulgar language is a distinctive trait of Chinese people today.

Because each side refuses to accept the other's point of view, each tries to cite the other as an embodiment of the evil times the world has fallen on and to blame them for their own misfortunes.

Some even dare to go from tongue lashings to fist fights, so runs the course of bloody incidents.

But who are the victims of these "evil times"? For instance, take Han Dongsheng — is he worse off now than he was ten years ago? And Xia Xiaoli — think of her lipstick, tweezers, earrings and necklace, the beauty parlour she goes to, the popular songs she listens to, the ice-cream sundaes she enjoys, the films (such as "Star Wars") she watches, and innumerable other diversions she enjoys. Aren't these all benefits of these "evil times"?

Almost every urban home in China has a number of electrical appliances now. There is even a widespread desire to acquire more durable goods and to discard out-of-date models for newer, better ones.

People complain about rising prices, yet continue to rush out and buy foodstuffs, clothing and household goods that were not even dreamed of in the past.

Even more important, the dark cloud of "class struggle" no longer hangs over everybody's head. Cadres no longer have to attend "May 7th cadre schools". Intellectuals are no longer automatically put in the "stinking ninth" category. One's brothers and sisters, sons and daughters are no longer hauled off to the countryside. People with a "bad class background" or "overseas relations" are not ostracized or exposed to public ridicule and persecution.

But no one seems to be satisfied!

A new set of conflicts has arisen to fill the gaps created by the economic reforms: between rich and poor, rich and richer, those who have gotten rich quick and those who have sweated long and hard for their wealth....

How to create harmony?

Trumpet forth selflessness and indifference to individual material benefits, kickbacks and perks. Stress the nobility of poverty, the worthiness of eschewing fame and wealth. Naturally, such virtues should be praised! But if the propaganda comes on too strong, it will surely raise doubts about the economic reforms. Encouraging people to associate material gain with their work is one of the most important psychological strategies of the current economic reform. But this smacks again of the "vicious circle" mentioned above.

The outcome of the current economic reforms will depend in great measure on the success or failure of each individual's psychological reform.

The essential thing is for people to nurture a sense of propriety. And the trick that will ensure success in putting theory into practice is a good mastery of balance.

Of course this is easier said than done.

The bus finally pulls away from the stop at Xidan.

How did this come about?

Just as things are at their most chaotic, an elderly gentleman in a Western-style suit emerges from the rear of the bus. He is tall and thin, with a set of sparse whiskers and a prominent Adam's apple.

Gesturing with his hands, he restrains several passengers who are locked in verbal combat with Xia Xiaoli, and turning to her he says gently, "Let's calm down now, shall we?"

Moving forward to the driver's seat, he says in an even more gentle voice to Han Dongsheng: "Young man, I can't speak for everybody; I'll just speak for myself. I think it would be best if we continued on the route. Don't you?"

It was that simple.

Han Dongsheng freezes. He is looking at the gentleman's eyes, at the look in those eyes.

What does he see in the man's expression?

Later, he can't say what it was. It is often impossible to explain one's thoughts.

But it is no accident that the look in the old man's eyes causes Han Dongsheng to think this way.

Sunday is Han Dongsheng's day off. The transportation team-leader encourages him to work overtime on Sundays, but he always refuses. He gets a bonus for working overtime, but it's only three *yuan*, so the prospect is unattractive. His favourite diversion on

Sundays is to bicycle with Jingjing to Zhongshan Park early in the morning. Jingjing rides a tiny bike with training wheels. Jingjing is really something: he's not even four yet, but he can ride all the way to the park, hugging the kerb, with his father shielding him from the traffic. That little bike cost Han Dongsheng fifty-six *yuan* — but he and Qin Shuhui had no qualms about spending it.

He will do anything for Jingjing. It costs one *yuan* to ride a little electric auto in the park for ten minutes; if it makes Jingjing happy, Han Dongsheng is willing to pay for several rides running. He also takes Jingjing to the Xidan Amusement Park, where the bumper cars cost two *yuan* for ten minutes. If it's two *yuan*, so be it; Jingjing, you wanna do it again?

Jingjing dresses as well as any rich kid. Mandarin oranges have just come on the market at three *yuan* per kilo. Han Dongsheng immediately buys two big ones for Jingjing, who will enjoy each and every slice by himself. We've said their family buys only half a kilo of mutton each month, but that's not quite accurate. Several times a month, they buy braised beef, a big chunk each time; this is consumed exclusively by Jingjing. Jingjing also has a considerable number of toys. When Han Dongsheng saw a new kind of vitamin E biscuit advertised on TV that was supposed to be good for brain development, Shuhui ran around half the city before she could find a box. Jingjing had not yet eaten all the biscuits when Han Dongsheng heard from someone in the transportation team that an excess of vitamin E can cause brain damage, whereupon he threw the unfinished biscuits into the rubbish bin without a second thought.

It is his feelings for Jingjing that cause Han Dongsheng to acquiesce to the look in the old gentleman's eyes.

These feelings not only connect him to Jingjing and Qin Shuhui; they connect him to his father-in-law, and to others as well.

His father-in-law is calling him. He goes over to see what he wants.

"My back, my back... "

He realizes the old man can't stand the pain; when he can tolerate it he doesn't call for help. Han Dongsheng massages his back. His father-in-law makes little noises — it's hard to tell whether they're cries of pain or pleasure.

The people in the compound all speak highly of Han Dongsheng and his wife. Everyone knows that Qin Shuhui is not the real daughter of this paralysed old man with his strange habits, but that he had adopted her when she was 56 days old. Han Dongsheng learned this during their courtship. He knows the whole story. Qin Shuhui's real mother is still alive, and they get together occasionally; both Qin and Han call her "Auntie". Auntie is the old man's sister-in-law; when her husband found out that his younger brother's wife was having difficulty getting pregnant, he gave his daughter to his brother for adoption. Qin Shuhui's uncle and adoptive mother are both dead now. Qin Shuhui and Han Dongsheng have impressed all the other residents of the compound by treating the paralysed old man like her real father. They have never been cruel to him.

This is not to say that Han Dongsheng and his wife have no misgivings on the subject. What the people in their compound — and of course the old man — don't know is that Han Dongsheng and Qin Shuhui once sought out a Legal Consultation Service Centre and asked questions like: since we're not blood relations, and since he has his own income, can we legally sever relations with him and arrange for him to live independently? Can't he use his income to hire someone to take care of him? Can't the government put him in a home for the aged? They were politely received at the consultation centre but after several hours of circuitous conversation they came away with a recommendation to maintain the status quo.

When they walked out of the consultation centre, Han Dong-sheng and Qin Shuhui's faces were flushed. On their way home, they bought five big imported bananas at three *yuan* per kilo without even discussing the purchase. When they got back they gave two bananas to Jingjing and three big ones to the old man.

By the door of their room in the courtyard, Han Dongsheng has built a tiny kitchen and a room some two metres square, where he used to store the paper boxes they were assembling. After their neighbour ratted on them, Han Dongsheng brought home an old oil drum from the bus company and installed it on the roof of the little room. He covered it with a pane of glass and led a pipe to it from the water main. And by installing another pipe with a faucet and shower head fed from the drum, he turned the room into an honest-to-goodness solar-heated shower. In the suffocating heat of summer, the sun warms the water in the drum to just the right temperature. From the end of June to the beginning of September, no one in the courtyard has to go to a public bath-house; they all use Han Dongsheng's solar shower....

So when Han Dongsheng saw the look in the eyes of the old gentleman who was counselling him to start the bus, he gave in.

Xia Xiaoli also has another side to her. Whenever she goes back to her parents' home in the outskirts of the city, she visits an old schoolmate, Chen Xuemei, who lives another two kilometres away. Because Xuemei's husband injured someone seriously in a fight, he has been sentenced to two years in jail. Now Xuemei and her daughter, who looks like a skinny cat, are struggling to make ends meet. Whenever Xia Xiaoli goes to see them, she helps her friend clean up the house and care for the child. When Xuemei weeps, Xia Xiaoli comforts her. When Xuemei says she wants a divorce, Xia Xiaoli reproaches her. With her arm around Xuemei's shoulder she talks to her like a best friend.

On her last visit, Xia Xiaoli gave Xuemei two bags of preserved prunes. Then she pulled out a photo of a young man from her beadwork wallet, and told Xuemei that she was the first person she had shown it to. This young man was a taxi driver in the company where Xia Xiaoli had worked briefly as a receptionist. Xuemei told her she should make up her mind about him quickly. Xia Xiaoli asked her for a cigarette; now it was Xuemei's turn to put her arm around her friend's shoulder while tears fell from Xia Xiaoli's eyes. Xuemei wiped them away with a handkerchief, her own voice breaking....

So when Xia Xiaoli sees the look in the old gentleman's eyes, she stops shouting at the passengers.

There is something impossible to describe in that look. It's something all too often missing from people's dealings with one another these days, something extremely rare and precious.

The old gentleman has been through a lot. He can always put himself in other people's shoes, and give the next guy the benefit of the doubt. For instance, take those two young toughs who tried to pick a fight with Han Dongsheng. Xia Xiaoli and Han Dongsheng detested them; and the bus passengers, the policeman and the neighbourhood security volunteers probably thought they were just a couple of no-good hooligans. Otherwise, why did they take off when the cops showed up?

But the old man takes a more tolerant view: they probably had something important to do, and were going to be late if they didn't get off at the Labour Union.

Maybe that's the way it was. Maybe the two of them with their blue jeans, ski sweaters, permed hair-dos and brass rings on their fingers actually had an extremely important piece of business to conduct. Perhaps they had an appointment with somebody and wanted to be prompt. Anticipating getting off at the Labour Union, they had sat in the last row of seats and hadn't heard the driver and ticket-seller when they had shouted, "First stop, Xidan!" When they had wanted to get off, the bus didn't stop and went straight to Xidan. Angry and disappointed, they felt that only a confrontation with the driver would restore a sense of equilibrium.

They aren't really out-and-out hoodlums. Maybe they just lack breeding; their language is crude, their movements rough — you might even describe them as repulsive. But they have their own lives to live and their own reasons for living. Naturally, they also have their problems; their lives are not easy. But few people think along these lines.

That elderly gentleman does.

He understands the driver even better, so he finds it easy to be tolerant and forgiving.

"Drivers don't have it easy," he tells a middle-aged woman standing next to him. "A while back, during the heat wave, I was on my way home with a bag full of things I'd bought in Wangfujing Street. The bus was crowded that day, and I'd been pushed all the way up to the front. My raffia bag was quite heavy, so I set it on the engine cover. When we got to this same stop, Xidan, my bag slipped sideways when the bus braked, spilling my things into the driver's compartment. The driver was a young man, too. First he glared at me, but then he picked up my things for me. When we got to Muxudi, I noticed that a room thermometer I had just bought was still on the floor of his compartment. I picked it up, sure that it had broken, but when I looked, it read forty-five degrees centigrade!"

The old gentleman's speech, delivered with true feeling, goes unheard by Han Dongsheng. Xia Xiaoli doesn't hear it either.

But they both feel and understand the look in the gentleman's eyes.

This incident took place in July, the hottest time of the year. The old gentleman was exhausted from shopping, but no one offered him a seat. Gripping the post supporting the partition behind the driver, he did his best to keep from falling. He thought about the time ten years before, during the last days of the Cultural Revolution, when a "service pledge" had been stencilled on the backs of the partitions in all the buses. Among the items was one that said, "We won't slam the door in your face or make you lose your footing." What sort of service is that? It's as if a restaurant were to put a big sign on the wall that says, "We promise not to poison you!" He glanced at the seats next to the ticket-seller labelled "Reserved for the elderly, the disabled, and pregnant women". An obese man was sitting there pretending to be asleep. The ticket-seller couldn't really get him to move, even though a mother carrying a toddler had just gotten on the bus. The woman sat the child on the ticket-seller's counter, but the ticket-seller did not feel this got in her way. This sort of scenario is re-enacted countless times every day on buses, and it helps dispel the temporary feeling of annoyance engendered by the likes of the overweight man. So the old gentleman did not curse his luck or express his resentment, but just stood there until the bus got to Muxudi and he retrieved his thermometer....

How true is the old saying, "You learn something new every day". Having taken buses for years, that was the first time he had realized the sort of conditions bus drivers work under in summer.

Seeing a lesson in every situation, seeing the whole in one of its parts, the look in his eyes gained strength and intensity.

No wonder when his eyes meet Han Dongsheng's they produce such an effect. Of course, Han Dongsheng cannot regain his equilibrium immediately. He decides to restart the bus. But he has to save face first. Turning to the passengers, he announces: "There's a mechanical problem. The battery's dead. If you want to move, you're all going to have to get out and push to get it started!"

All the passengers start jabbering at once. No one believes him. No one wants to get off and push. Some click their tongues in derision; others look as if they're going to start another argument.

But the old gentleman steps off the bus, saying, "Let's give it a push! It'll be good exercise!"

Several people go, then a dozen. Finally everybody gets off and starts pushing. Xia Xiaoli sticks her head out of a side window and calls to the old gentleman: "Get away from there, old man! Let them push!"

Han Dongsheng starts up the bus. Everybody gets back on, someone giving the old gentleman a hand up the stairs. Another person offers him a seat, which he accepts.

Finally, the bus is on its way to the next stop.

Buses, buses, buses.

You will meet drivers like Han Dongsheng and ticket-sellers like Xia Xiaoli on Peking buses. You may often have to share one square metre of space with a dozen other Chinese people, "building a Great Wall of flesh and blood".[5]

Think about it for a moment: perhaps "We have built a new Great Wall of our flesh and blood" is a figure of speech better applied to more significant events. But if we don't try to make comparisons like this, what else can we do?

First completed 1 October 1985, Chinese National Day
Revised 19 October 1985

---

[5] A line from the Chinese national anthem.

The Woman with
Shoulder-length Hair

He first saw her on Sunlight Rock.

Sunlight Rock is the highest point on Gulangyu Island, and offers a view of the entire Xiamen Peninsula, as well as the two smaller islands of Dadan and Erdan.

You can rent binoculars on Sunlight Rock, ten *fen* for five minutes. The woman who runs the concession measures the time with an alarm clock she holds in her hand. It rings once every five minutes.

He wanted to rent them, but somebody else there was using them.

When he glanced over to to see who it was, he could feel his heart pounding in his chest.

She was a young woman, about his age, with a lovely slim figure. Some people say Xiamen girls are the best-dressed in China. Even the most fashionable girls on the Bund in Shanghai or Haizhu Plaza in Guangzhou can't compare with them. There are several reasons for this: first, Xiamen women make their clothing from better material, much of it imported from Hong Kong, Macao or abroad; secondly, Xiamen women know how to mix and match the colours of what they wear. A Xiamen girl might wear something as bright as autumn leaves one day, and something as subdued as a wisp of smoke the next. Or she'll do something whimsical, like putting a striking V-neck in a formal and elegant dress, or harmonizing two contrasting colours with a carefully chosen belt.... The woman with the binoculars was wearing the simplest light-green dress without a single accessory, yet she looked as charming and pretty as could be. Taking a closer look, he realized that the real source of her beauty was her thick, luxuriant shoulder-length hair. She wore it loose without hairclips, and he watched as it rose and fell gently in the breeze, glowing in the sunlight.

She had the binoculars aimed at a particular spot, and didn't move them from there. This was the tip of egret-shaped Xiamen Island, the so-called Egret's Beak. He wondered what mysterious thing there she found so enticing.

While she was looking off into the distance, he was examining her from close up. None of the Chinese or foreign tourists milling around the rock paid any attention to them. In fact, the only one who seemed to care at all was the woman in charge of the binoculars, who watched the two of them without the slightest hint of emotion. Though she was young, the proprietor of the binoculars was something of an anomaly in Xiamen: there was nothing remarkable about her looks, and she was wearing the most conventional clothing.

The alarm sounded. Five minutes was up. The woman with the shoulder-length hair put down the binoculars with some reluctance. The woman in charge said to her: "Give them to him."

He waved his hand in refusal and said: "That's all right, I don't want them."

The woman in charge was a bit surprised by this. The woman with shoulder-length hair casually handed the binoculars to the man without even glancing at him, and then started down the stairs of Sunlight Rock.

The staircase was very narrow, and there were people climbing up from below. Every few seconds she had to squeeze to the side in order to let the others pass. Every time she did this, her splendid black hair bounced up and down in the most seductive fashion.

He followed her with his eyes. When she disappeared around the corner of a wall of rock that led to the Cave for Avoiding Summer Heat, he too started down the narrow staircase. As he descended, he bumped into some of the people who were on their way up, and they clicked their tongues disapprovingly as he passed by.

After making his way down the narrow staircase he came to a broader path, and strode quickly through the cool shadows of the Cave for Avoiding Summer Heat, searching for her.

In less than a minute, he had lost her.

This left him depressed and disappointed.

He was twenty-six, and needed a steady "her" in his life. With his good family background and excellent qualifications, numerous "hers" had come knocking on his door hoping that he would accept their favours. His mother had even picked out a "her" for him, the youngest daughter of one of his parents' old friends. He had nothing against this particular "her", an intelligent girl studying to be an ear, nose and throat specialist. They had similar family backgrounds, and her job prospects were excellent. They had spent a lot of time together in the past, and had always gotten along quite well. Logically speaking, the question of his marriage should have been resolved by now, but he simply refused to commit himself. His indecisiveness gave his mother angina pains every time she thought about it. With the utmost seriousness, his parents had asked him: "What's wrong with her?" When he broke down and told them the truth, they gave him a severe dressing down.

He asked himself: What have I done wrong?

He had come to Xiamen on business. There, he hoped, he would meet the woman of his dreams. He was leaving the next day. Just as he was about to give up hope, this beauty with her shoulder-length hair had appeared before him, as fresh as a pale-green chrysanthemum.

He was especially fond of all those ancient and modern stories about love at first sight. He was confident that before long scientists would explain this phenomenon, one of life's great mysteries, in the following manner: Love at first sight is simply a powerful physiological response that occurs between two particular individuals of the opposite sex. To hell with all dumb sociological explanations, and pedantic psychoanalytical inquiries into human emotions!

Clearly there was some inexplicable natural force linking him with this woman with the shoulder-length hair. Now that they had found each other, he couldn't let her go.

Quickening his pace, he entered the Sunlight Temple and found himself among the crowd of tourists there. A number of worshippers — he wondered whether they were true devotees or not — enveloped in a cloud of incense were bowing to the Goddess of Mercy on the altar known as the One-tile Shrine. Glancing in that direction, he was much relieved to discover that she was not among them. He left the temple through the main entrance and continued down the hill.

When the mountain path took a turn, he finally caught sight of her, gracefully winding her way down the mountain. As the wind caught the hem of her light-green skirt and lifted it gently, he could see her slender legs and dainty feet, shod in a pair of pearly-white high heels. She had a creme-coloured vinyl purse with a silver clasp slung over her right shoulder. Raising her elbows slightly, she put her hands on her bag to prevent it from swinging about. Still the most striking thing about her was her shoulder-length hair, which rose and fell in gentle ripples...

As he followed after her, he could feel his heart pounding in his chest. Obviously this was not only due to the steepness of the descent. Camel Hump Peak was not very high, and she made it down to the bottom quickly, and paused under a clump of plum trees, wondering where to go next. From this he concluded that she had come to Xiamen as a tourist, and thus had plenty of free time on her hands. As far as he was concerned, this was ideal.

She stood there for a few seconds, then turned and sat down on a stone bench in the shade of a plum tree. Raising her head, she gently arranged her splendid hair. As he watched her, his blood turned to wine.

This was his big chance. Boldly, even rudely, he forced himself into her consciousness: he walked up to her and said, still out of breath: "Let's...let's get to know each other, OK?"

She stood up with a start, and instinctively turned away from him.

"Excuse me, I'm terribly sorry, really..." he added quickly. "Please don't be afraid, I'm not going to hurt you. I just... I just thought I'd like to get to know you."

When she turned to look at him, he saw her face was pale with fright. She gave him an angry look, but at the same time, she noticed him blushing in embarrassment, saw that his eyes were filled with guilt and remorse, and that he had his arms crossed in front of his chest — he hardly seemed like the sort of person who could harm her. She stood there, not moving, as the colour gradually returned to her cheeks, and the animosity in her eyes gave way to scrutiny. It took her a few more seconds to recover completely, whereupon she said to him coolly: "Who are you? What do you want from me?"

He started to explain, but later, after it was all over, he couldn't recall what he had said to her. He was thinking that her face wasn't beautiful in the usual sense, and was actually flawed in several respects: she had big eyes, but her cheek-bones seemed a touch too broad; her nose was straight and long, but her chin was a bit pointed; and she had freckles alongside her nose. In sum, the overall impression was one of flawed beauty. Yet combine this face with her gorgeous shoulder-length hair, and she could very well pass for an angel.

And then, believe it or not, this blessed angel smiled at him, though this vague, barely perceptible movement of the lips — she didn't even show her teeth — could hardly be called a proper smile. But for him it was quite enough.

And so this is how he got to know her. Or perhaps it would be more accurate to say that this is how she permitted him to get to know her.

They went to the Shuzhuang Garden. From the famous Forty-four Zig-zag Bridge they listened to the waves breaking on the rocks below, and followed the seagulls circling over the water. The more they talked, the closer they became. Alas, why hadn't they met earlier?

Naturally, they began their conversation with the sights of Gulangyu, and then went on to their favourite movies, novels, and poems. Was it mere coincidence that they both preferred the Shuzhuang Garden to Sunlight Rock, agreed that Liu Xiaoqing was a better actress than Joan Chen, thought Victor Hugo was a better novelist than Balzac, and disliked Walt Whitman's *Leaves of Grass*? And was it by dint of Fate that they both could recite this passage from Longfellow by heart:

Be still, sad heart! and cease repining;
Behind the clouds is the sun still shining;
Thy fate is the common fate of all,
Into each life some rain must fall,

Some days must be dark and dreary.

After making their way across the Forty-four Zig-zag Bridge, they sat down for a rest in the Pavilion of Cool Breezes, climbed up Grass-seed Hill, and entered Bushan Garden. They strolled slowly in the shade of the palm trees, breathing in the scent of the magnolias, chatting about everything under the sun, until they came to the famous Twelve Caves Leading to Heaven. This was a large walk-in rockery built in the style of the classical gardens of Suzhou. Here the designer had managed to create the illusion of great depth and complexity within a limited space; the rocks gave whoever walked through them a feeling of profound serenity and fulfilment.

He asked her to explore the maze-like rockery with him. She hesitated before the entrance.

"No", she said, looking him in the eye and drawing back a few steps. "I can't."

"Why not?" He looked right at her, wondering why she had changed her mind so suddenly.

"I just don't feel like going in there." Suddenly she looked inscrutable to him.

"Are you scared?" He thought for a moment, then turned away and said, "That's all right, we don't have to go into the 'Twelve Caves Leading to Heaven.' You must be tired now. Let's go over there and rest for a while."

She nodded and they started to retrace their steps. They sat down on a cracked stone bench in the shade of a pine tree. He gazed at her with a searching look in his eyes. She lowered her head, and her hair spread evenly over the back of her neck. From where he was sitting, her eyelashes looked especially long. Nervously she toyed with the creme-coloured handbag on her knees, her lips tightly pursed.

"Is anything the matter?" he asked her timidly.

"This is the first time I've ever been with a stranger," she said softly.

He didn't want to lie to her. This wasn't the first time for him. But he wished it *was* the first time, and the last time as well.

"I'm afraid of being cheated. I'm even more afraid I might cheat someone…"

"Don't say things like that," he said, and began to tell her about himself. "I'm not a playboy. I'm a very serious guy. It's still hard for me to believe…you know…what a coincidence it was that we met… I'm going back to Peking tomorrow. I really hope we can stay in touch. I'll give you my address at work, and at home… I'm going to tell my parents all about you…"

"How much do you know about me?" she said, raising her head. She avoided looking at him, knitted her eyebrows, and fixed her gaze on some weeds on the nearby slope.

"Of course, we have to get to know each other better. But, but I… like you for what you are, and that's enough for me. Is there something about you that's going to scare me away?"

"Yes, and…"

"Whatever it is I don't give a damn!" he said with supreme self-confidence. "Believe me, I'm not the kind of guy who gets uptight about petty things."

"Do you want to know what my job is?"

"I don't care what you do. I don't even care if you're unemployed."

"I'm a waitress in a restaurant. Remember you asked me what I was looking at with the binoculars on Sunlight Rock? I was trying to find the restaurant I work in. I found it finally."

"I don't care if you're a waitress in a restaurant. Really. That's not important. Anyway, we'll get you a new job in Peking… If you don't want to work, it doesn't matter. We both like Longfellow's poetry, right? That's enough for me."

"I've got relatives overseas."

"That's great! Most people I know would give their right arm to have relatives overseas. What's wrong with that? Things aren't the way they were four years ago…"

"I have an aunt in Hong Kong. She sells satay noodles in the street. She's not one of those rich types that can afford to bring tape recorders and television sets to her relatives in China every time she comes. When I asked her to buy something for me in Hong Kong, it turned out to be a terrible burden for her, she even had to borrow money from someone, and I didn't get it until last year. Do you know what she bought me?"

"Let's not waste time talking about things like that. I don't care what she bought you. All we need from your aunt is her blessing, that's all, we don't need any gifts…"

"My health isn't very good…"

"You can do something about that…"

"I've been seriously ill. When I was sent down to the country-side, I nearly died once."

"But you recovered, didn't you? Of course you did, and now look how beautiful you are…"

"Don't say things like that. There's something I haven't told you, one of the after-effects…"

"So what? I swear to you, even if we can't have children, I'll never regret marrying you."

What he said surprised her, and now she turned to look at him. There were tears in her eyes, and she was blushing. She bit her lower lip and remained silent for a while.

He said, "Let's walk a bit. Why do we have to talk about such painful things? We can discuss all of this later in our letters." She stood up without replying.

They left the Shuzhuang Garden and strolled along Back-bay Beach. It was late autumn: the leaves on the trees were a deep green, and here and there clumps of flowers showed their colours, but no one was swimming. As the sun set, brilliant purple and red clouds edged in silver hovered near the horizon. The tide was receding slowly, and the waves breaking on the shore drew undulating lines of foam across the surface of the water. The evening breeze was perfumed with the humid scent of cassia blossoms, both refreshing and intoxicating.

She kept her head down as she walked slowly along the beach. The breeze stirred her light green skirt, and lifted her beautiful black hair.

They walked shoulder to shoulder. He glanced at her from time to time, taking pleasure in her slender profile, and especially in her hair blowing in the breeze. How he wished he could link arms with her, and feel the tenderness of her skin; how he wished he could caress her soft, lustrous hair. But he stopped at going that far.

Suddenly she turned around, narrowed her eyes and stared at him. He felt she was looking right through him. She said, "Tell me, what do you see in me?"

"You're my ideal woman. I swear to God, I've seen you in my dreams…"

"Lay off the flowery stuff. I think it's because you think…you like my body."

"Of course I love the way you look, but it's you, your soul, I love even more!"

"We've only been together for a couple of hours. How can either of us know anything about the other's soul?"

"You're absolutely right. That's why we have to stay in touch and write to each other often. And find a way to meet again…"

She knitted her eyebrows so intensely that they began to twitch. He wondered why this was so painful for her, why she seemed so worried. If she really wasn't the romantic type, why had she spent the last few hours alone with him?

"I have to get back to Xiamen. What about you?" she said coolly, with a sigh.

"I'm staying here on the island, but I'll see you off at the ferry dock. When we get there I hope you'll give me your address."

He had told her his address when they had left the Shuzhuang Garden, but he wanted to write it down for her so she wouldn't forget it.

She said nothing and let him see her off. The dock was swarming with people. After a long day of sightseeing on the island, the tired tourists were all there waiting for the ferry to take them back to Xiamen for dinner. There was a billboard on the dock, perhaps with a huge advertisement for TDK cassette tapes. But they didn't notice this, and kept their eyes fixed on each other.

"They say that officials' sons like you only go for women with good family connections, or girls with beautiful bodies…"

"I'm not that kind of guy, let me tell you…"

"Let me tell *you*, if a guy like that marries a girl with a similar background, he'll lose interest soon and start going after other girls to get his kicks. And if he just marries a girl for her looks, he may treat her well for a while, but actually he won't have any respect for her…"

"What do you want me to do then, rip my chest open and show you my heart?"

She smiled at him, a sad and elusive smile. "No, you don't have to do that. It's all very simple. Here, take this. I wrote it a long time ago in case I ran into someone like you. I wrote it so guys like you might think twice the next time…"

She removed a sealed envelope from her bag.

When he reached out to take it, she instinctively drew back her hand. Glancing at the dock, she handed it to him, and said rather seriously: "Please don't open it until the ferry's half way across the harbour."

Then she started running towards the dock, without looking back once. He watched her force her way through the crowd and make her way onto the boat. He could still see her shoulder-length hair, glowing in the sunset....

Like a fool he stood there clutching the envelope in his hand with all his might. The ferry glided away from the dock, made a slow turn, and headed for Xiamen.

He thought he might be able to get a final glimpse of her shoulder-length hair among all the other heads on the boat. But he couldn't find her. Was she trying to avoid him? Didn't she want to watch his reaction when he opened the letter?

The sky had turned dark and gloomy. The strong smell of the sea only intensified his longing.

He did as she said and only opened the letter after the ferry had gone more than half way across the harbour.

He read the letter:

> *Perhaps I will never be able to find happiness in this world, because there is something I must confess to you: When I had typhoid fever, I lost all of my hair. My wig and false eyelashes were a gift to me from my poor, hard-working aunt in Hong Kong. If you really are the kind of man you claim to be, I want to hear from you again. Please write to me at...*

He stopped reading there.

When the lights on the dock came on, the elderly woman selling bananas and tangerines watched as a fashionably dressed young man tore up a piece of paper and tossed the shreds into the sea.

26 November 1980
Written after a journey to Gulangyu

The Wish

It was exercise time in the editorial room, but as usual, although work had stopped, no one was doing their exercises. Somebody was holding forth in a loud voice about some amusing episode, and had just elicited a great burst of laughter when my telephone rang. Amidst all the racket, it was impossible to hear clearly what was being said at the other end of the line. In response to my shouts and gestures the hubbub did subside somewhat, however, and I was finally able to make out that the person calling me was Cao, the party secretary at the middle school where I had once taught. We'd had very little to do with each other in the three years since I'd been transferred to the publishing house, largely because we'd both been so busy; but in fact while I'd still been at the school we'd been very close.

"What's up, Cao?" I asked in a loud voice, my mouth pressed

The Chinese title of this story, *"Ruyi"*, means literally, "as you wish"; *ruyi* is also the name of an S-shape sceptre-like ornamental object, often of jade or other precious materials, formerly given as a present among the Chinese to signify wishes for the good fortune of the recipient.

close to the receiver. He hadn't changed a bit. Regardless of however tragic or happy the occasion, he never allowed it to have the slightest effect on his outward demeanour. In a slow and relaxed voice, but straight to the point, he said:

"Old Uncle Shi Yihai from the school has died. We're going to hold a memorial meeting, and after a lot of thought we've decided that you ought to be the one to write the speech."

The racket going on all around me seemed suddenly to fade into the distance, and I felt my heart sink like a lead weight. Grasping the receiver tightly, I felt my throat tighten. My voice sounded strange:

"When did he die?"

Cao's reply was brief and to the point.

"The day before yesterday. He died on the way to the hospital, a heart attack. We've cleared up his things, what there were of them that is, you know what a simple life he led. But we found a parcel in that wooden chest of his, a thick parcel, wrapped up very tightly …"

"What was in it?" I asked impatiently, unable to restrain myself. Cao told me. Drawing in my breath, I felt as if I could hear a vast orchestra of Chinese lutes, "their thick strings fiercely thrummed, like a squall of rain", as the poet has it, and I couldn't help murmuring out loud to myself, "So that's what it was!"

I was deeply shaken. The memorial meeting was fixed for the following afternoon, and I agreed to write a speech that night and take the next day off so that I could deliver it to the school and participate in the ceremony.

That evening as I sat at my desk I forgot about everything except Uncle Shi — we had always addressed him as Uncle out of respect for his age. It was an autumn night, calm and tranquil as only an autumn night can be. You could almost hear the sound of leaves falling from distant trees. All of my sorrow seemed poised at the tip of my pen, but still, for a time, I didn't know where to begin.

Silently, I invoked him. Uncle Shi, if you have a soul, then ride on the gentle breeze, and in the stillness of the night come to my side, so that once again we can sit huddled together, holding nothing back from each other. I miss you, Uncle Shi. Do you miss me, too? You probably do. Oh, Uncle Shi!

I

I started work at the school in 1961. Many of the young teachers at that time actually lived at the school, and every morning, our ablutions completed, whether we were jogging on the exercise ground, reciting texts from memory underneath a tree, or making our way to the office to prepare the day's lessons, we would always see, through the fine mist or bathed in the glow of dawn, a worker in his fifties, sweeping the school grounds with a big bamboo broom. He wasn't tall, but he was thickset with broad shoulders, while his legs were very markedly bowed. Methodically and rhythmically he would sweep away, stroke after stroke, slowly and silently making his way forward, his head bowed. Whenever I saw him I would think to myself vaguely, "Ah, there goes Uncle Shi sweeping again," but the thought was never more than a single flimsy strand of gossamer floating in the breeze, which vanished into thin air as soon as he disappeared from sight. The other resident teachers more or less took the same attitude towards him.

I should make it clear, however, that my attitude (and that of my colleagues) should in no way be interpreted as arising out of snobbish disdain for a worker. Uncle Ge, for example, a tall, thin fellow with sunken cheeks who was in charge of the reception office, was several years older than Shi. Apparently prior to Liberation he'd been a Taoist monk, and we often teased him in a friendly way about it. He was quite well read, and was very diligent in his distribution of newspapers, letters and remittances. He also liked engaging us in conversation about current affairs. Uncle Shi, on the other hand, was quite illiterate, hence unqualified to work in the reception office, and there just didn't seem to be any natural links between him and us. When you added to this the fact that he was extremely taciturn by nature, and had a totally expressionless face, it was really little wonder that he failed to attract our attention.

It was not until the May Day Festival of 1962 that I had my first rather remarkable personal and private contact with Uncle Shi. As I was on patrol duty, I hadn't gone off to take part in the festivities, but instead had remained behind at the school where it was my job to walk around the high walls of the exercise ground once every hour. Uncle Shi lived in a little single-storey house situated in a corner of the exercise ground, and it was there that I passed the time when I wasn't off on my rounds. To start with I simply sat and occupied myself with the novel which I'd brought with me, paying no attention to Uncle Shi, who was sitting on the bed rubbing leaf tobacco for his pipe. Each time I sat down and began to read, though, he would silently pour me another cup of tea, and I began to feel slightly embarrassed. The third time I came back from my patrol I put the book to one side, and racking my brain for something to say, endeavoured to start a conversation.

I remembered having heard the headmaster tell us that the school was built on the site of what had once been a prince's mansion. Thinking that such a residence could hardly have had an exercise ground such as we now had, I asked casually:

"Uncle Shi, do you know what the exercise ground originally was when this was still a prince's mansion?"

"Of course. It was a garden."

Immediately a series of images from *The Dream of the Red Chamber* appeared in my mind's eye, in particular — I don't know why —

from chapter 101, "A ghostly warning is given on a moonlit night in Prospect Garden." So naturally, as any other young person would have done, I went on to ask the old man sitting in front of me whether or not the garden was haunted.

"Of course it's haunted. I've seen the ghost myself," replied Uncle Shi calmly, as if it were a perfectly normal occurrence, and continued puffing away rhythmically on his six-inch pipe.

"I don't believe it. Ghosts don't exist, surely?"

"You don't believe it? But I've seen it with my own eyes."

"It must have been an optical illusion. There are no such things as ghosts."

"No such things? But I've seen one."

Once again, like most young people receiving such a reply, I asked, only half wishing to hear the answer,

"Really? Then what did it look like, this ghost you saw?"

Raising his head slightly so as to meet my eyes, his full, round face still devoid of any sign of unusual emotion, he replied:

"I was only about the age you are now, I reckon. The better half of the prince's mansion had already been given over to the missionary school. The exercise ground wasn't as big as it is now, and there was a dormitory row in the eastern half. At night the pupils used to piss into big wooden buckets, which would all be put up at the far end of the dormitory block. It used to be my job to empty them out, and sometimes I'd do it as early as four in the morning. One day — I think the weather was probably pretty much like it is now — I got up a bit earlier than usual and headed off for the dormitory. I was just about there when all of a sudden I saw the flash of a white figure. Proper queer I thought it was. It looked like a girl's figure, in a white blouse and a black skirt. Now you know our school's always been for boys only, so what in heaven's name was a girl doing, suddenly rushing out in the middle of the night?"

Wishing to display my scepticism, and to give my courage a

boost at the same time, I made a stab at an explanation:

"Some girls are brazen enough, she must have got in over the wall."

"No, no," Uncle Shi replied, his tone still perfectly calm and unruffled. "I went across to her and called out, 'Don't hide, come on out!' And out she came from the corner — jet black hair, face as white as snow, her eyes drooping at the corners and her lips as red as if they were bleeding."

"That was no ghost," I interrupted, "that was a real live person." Uncle Shi pressed on with his story as if he hadn't heard me.

"I stood there, face to face with her. I asked her, 'Are you a devil or a human being? Tell me!' Then she bowed to me. She was crying, and said, 'Elder brother, I'm a human being, not a devil.'"

At this he paused. Feeling my heart contract, I didn't take my eyes off him. He took another puff on his pipe, and continued:

"I was just puzzling over what it was all about, when she added, 'What a miserable fate is mine.' And then she turned around and walked away. I watched her go, bare-footed, and it looked as though her feet were at least an inch above the ground, almost flickering they were, then she went round the corner of the building and was gone."

My hair was on end, and my ears were full of the amplified sound of my own heart beating. A shiver of unease ran up my spine. I was suddenly afraid of going out on my next patrol.

It took me quite a few minutes to calm myself down. But, after all, I was a member of the Communist Youth League, and it was my duty to be a good materialist; I had no business allowing myself to be infected by the poison of superstition. Putting on a serious expression, I told Uncle Shi:

"You are definitely the victim of a hallucination. There are no such things as ghosts — no such things."

Uncle Shi was incredibly stubborn. He continued puffing away at his pipe, his expression unchanged, and it was not until several minutes had passed that he countered:

"How could I have been seeing things? Afterwards, I felt sorry for her. I reckoned she must have been suffering from some injustice or something, so I secretly bought a pair of stockings and in the middle of the night I put them on the spot where I'd met her. When it got light I went to have a look, and they were gone. None of the pupils were up yet, so no one could have taken them but her. And that was the last time she ever appeared. She'd probably got her revenge, I suppose."

By now even the fine hair on my back was standing on end, and for a time I was lost for words with which to refute him.

"You have a break, I'll go out and take a turn for you." Uncle Shi stood up, and taking the torch from the table, ambled out of the room. I pressed my spine up against the wall, struggling to hold down the fear welling up inside me. I was furious at Uncle Shi for his superstition and his stubbornness, but at the same time I was grateful for his kindness and consideration.

However, once the night had passed, in the full light of the following day, the only impression of him that remained with me was a negative one, of backwardness and obstinacy. After that, I kept my contacts with Uncle Shi to a minimum.

II

I didn't re-establish a relationship with Uncle Shi until the autumn of 1964. By that time the school had already adopted the then current practice of holding meetings to listen to recollections by workers and peasants of the bitter lives they led before the revolution, of ceremonially eating miserable meals of the sort which had once been their lot, of interviewing people who had been especially disadvantaged in pre-Liberation times, and the like.

One day I went to call on Cao. At that time he'd only just been assigned to the school as deputy Party secretary, and although he was no more than thirty-eight, his dark, gaunt appearance, then as now, made him look much older. I started to complain straight-away.

"What activities have you got in mind for the pupils now? We've already eaten two 'recalling bitterness meals'!"

"We could organize more meetings..." he replied somewhat hesitantly.

"We've already interviewed all the typical representatives around here," I said, raising my voice, "If we have to go further afield, we'll have to give up even more class time. Are we going to allow the pupils to do any regular study or not?"

"Actually, there's someone we could interview right here at the school," said Cao, inclining his head to one side.

"Who's that?" I asked impatiently. When he mentioned Uncle Shi, I was flabbergasted.

"Him?"

Cao nodded.

"I've read his file, and I've been over to his place to chat with him. He was born around the time of the 1911 Revolution — a foundling brought up in a church orphanage. His parents must have been urban poor who had no way of providing for him, so they abandoned him. Pretty lucky, really, surviving to grow up in an orphanage with nothing the worse to show except his bandy legs. When he was ten or thereabouts he was taken in as a servant by a priest at the mission school. Ever since he was a child he had to wait on the foreign devils, taking their beatings and abuse as well as doing all the hardest and dirtiest jobs. And so it went, right up to Liberation. It wasn't until 1952, when the school was taken over by the government and the foreign priests packed their bags and went off with their tails between their legs, that he finally began to lead a life free of exploitation and oppression. I think you ought to get him to tell the pupils about his bitter past. It's quite likely that the kids will be more deeply moved by the personal testimony of a janitor right here at their own school than if we invited someone from outside."

Actually I'd had no idea that Uncle Shi's was such a classic "history of blood and tears". In accordance with Cao's suggestion, I went over to Uncle Shi's lodgings to see him. When I entered the room, he was preparing himself a pot of plain wheat-dumpling soup. I explained the reason for my visit, and because I was afraid he might refuse, I concluded by emphasizing that I had come at the urging of the Party branch.

Holding the dough in his hand, Uncle Shi stopped tearing off the strips of dough as he listened to what I had to say, and let the water boil away unattended, although his face showed no trace of any emotion. However, to my surprise, he happily acceded to my request without the slightest hesitation.

"Fine, I'll give a talk then."

He came to the classroom to make his speech. At first, although his delivery was a bit wooden, he spoke fully in accordance with what was expected of him, and his tone of voice was very sincere:

"You don't know how lucky you are to be living now — you've got no idea how the foreigners used to push us around in the old days…"

I felt a deep sense of satisfaction as I watched the pupils fixing their gaze on him, hanging on his every word. After he'd been speaking for ten minutes or so, though, it became pretty obvious that there was quite a difference in the way Uncle Shi judged and felt about the two foreign priests who used to work at the school.

"You know that trap-door in classroom 3B that's fastened down with a padlock? The foreigners really knew how to enjoy themselves in those days. Underneath it there's a flight of stairs leading down to a cellar, and they had case after case of beer which they'd imported from the land of Oulouba (that's actually how he referred to Europe!) stacked away down there. Whenever they felt like a drop, they'd send me down to fetch some. Well, the hotter it was, the more they'd tend to drink, naturally, so at the height of summer I'd be up and down ten times a day if it was once. That Master De (he was referring to Father De Taibai, which was the Chinese name the priest had chosen for himself), we servants used to call him 'Bread' behind his back, he was as white as a peeled potato and as fat as a gourd. He was just as lazy and just as much of an exploiter as any of your typical foreigners, but he did treat you pretty much like a human being, and when he told you to do something he was always very polite. 'Yihai,' he'd say, 'would you get me another bottle of beer please?' And when I'd given it to him, he'd nod to me and say thank you. If he happened to be in a good mood, he might even let me finish off what was in the bottle after he'd poured himself a good glass.

"But that swine Master He (here he was referring to the priest known in Chinese as Father He Ai'er), now he was terrible, another kettle of fish altogether, the nickname we had for him was 'Carrot' — he had a brandy nose that really was redder than a carrot. There was no end to the airs he put on when he started to boss you around. 'Fetch my beer!', he'd yell, and we'd hurry off to the cellar, tripping over ourselves in the rush. If you were even just a bit slow you were quite likely to get a clip over the ear. Once, I'd just come up from the cellar, and for some reason the hand that I was holding the bottle with wouldn't stop shaking. Well, Carrot glared at me and bawled me out: 'What the bloody hell's the matter with you? What've you been up to to get the shakes like that?' The beggar really had the Peking slang off pat, he was a tricky customer to deal with. I simply replied, 'I was in a muck sweat from today's heat, and going down into the cellar all of a sudden the cool air just started me shaking naturally, I couldn't help it.' He thought I was answering him back, and wouldn't be content until he'd punished me by making me go back down into the cellar and stay there for an hour. I pleaded with him, but it wasn't any use, he pushed and shoved me back down there and then he slammed the trap-door shut and locked it. I only had a thin shirt on, and in the cold of the cellar my top teeth seemed to be fighting a battle with the bottom ones. But thanks to Bread doing the decent thing, I was let out before the hour was up. I heard him going on at Carrot, telling him how he was cruel and acting against the will of God. Carrot was arguing back, but Bread continued to stick up for me…"

Well, you can imagine the mounting anxiety with which I listened as Uncle Shi came out with such a succession of highly suspect utterances. The pupils, on the other hand, were entranced, and from time to time whispered amongst themselves. Unable to tolerate the situation, I seized the opportunity provided by my going up to pour him a glass of water to interject, seemingly naturally:

"The two priests were in fact the same in nature. Bread was actually more sinister than Carrot because of his deceitfulness. All crows in the world are black!"

But despite the fact, known to everyone, that this last common expression was much favoured by Chairman Mao in describing similar situations, to my amazement, stupid old Uncle Shi turned to me and said:

"Not all crows are black. Actually, there's one in the garden at the rear of the residence with a grey throat and a white belly."

The pupils burst out with a great roar of laughter. White with anger, I spilt the water which I was pouring into his tea cup all over the table. I silently cursed Cao — he should never have come up with such a daft idea. What a speaker to have recommended! One who actually went so far as to disagree with the universally accepted crow maxim. Once this was over I'd have the devil of a job cleaning up the poison that had been spread about.

Worried that what he would say next might be even more out of line, I proffered a bit of guidance:

"Apart from recalling your own bitterness, you can tell us something about when this school was still a prince's mansion, so that we can learn about the tragic oppression of the servants."

He cleared his throat, and after reflecting for a moment began:

"All sorts of awful things happened in the mansion. Quite apart from anything else, I heard tell of a whole number of servant girls who finished themselves off by throwing themselves down the well. What was so bad about their lives that they'd want to do a thing like that? They were violated by the prince, that's what. Later on the garden was destroyed and the well filled up, but their wronged spirits continued to linger about the place. I myself saw…"

I realized we were in trouble, and terrified that he was going to tell all these "flowers of the Motherland" a ghost story of the sort he'd told me, I immediately cut in:

"What a lot of things you know, Uncle Shi. Actually, you don't have to restrict yourself to telling us about the mansion — you can also tell us about the miserable lives led by the poor people who lived in this neighbourhood in the old society."

Sinking half the cup of the tea in one gulp, he launched into the topic:

"If someone's poor, he's sure as anything to get kicked around. There were any number of poor people around here who used to be bullied and suffer hardships. Just south of the school here, for instance, the Jin sisters at number 14 Bamboo Leaf Lane, they really suffered. If they hadn't looked after one another so well, and then had the good fortune to be able to enter the new society, who knows what sort of a hole they'd have finished up in, leaving their ghosts behind?"

Ghosts again! I realized that if I didn't cut him off, we were going to be in still more trouble, so taking advantage of this pause in the flow of words I announced:

"Uncle Shi is an old man and hasn't been in very good health recently, so we'll stop here today. Let's give Uncle Shi a good round of applause for the very vivid lesson that he's taught us."

We saw him off to the sound of clapping.

When I'd used the expression "vivid lesson" I was doing no more than repeating the usual cliche; but it seemed that as far as the pupils were concerned, it really had been vivid. For days afterwards they discussed Bread and Carrot, and the Jin sisters also aroused great interest. A week later, the little cadres of the class committee made the following report to me:

"Everyone in the class suggests that we invite the two Jin sisters, known for their great suffering and deep hatred, to address us on the subject of their bitter past."

As it happened, I'd been at a loss as to how to arrange further educational activities, so after some thought, I agreed. Armed with a letter of introduction, I set out in person to make the necessary arrangements. I thought that on this occasion I should make absolutely certain just what sort of people they were. If they turned out to be as muddle-headed as Uncle Shi, then no matter how bitter a family history they had, I was not going to invite them to address us.

III

When I called on the Neighbourhood Committee the chair-woman was absent, so — perhaps a little presumptuously — I went directly to number 14. It was a small courtyard residence inhabited by six households. Around 1964, before the housing problem really reached the explosive proportions which it later assumed, the practice of cluttering up the courtyards with makeshift sheds and extra rooms had not yet become widespread; in appearance, therefore, it gave an impression of spaciousness despite its small size. It was, moreover, decorated all about with flowers and plants, and although the building was old, it was clean and well kept.

It turned out that the Jin sisters were both about fifty. They lived separately, one on the south side of the courtyard, the other on the north, each occupying only one room. I entered the southern room first; seated inside was a burly chap with a sallow complexion whom I recognized as a senior worker who manufactured briquettes at the nearby coal depot. After exchanging a few words with him I realized that he was the husband of the younger of the two sisters. He told me that "the missus", a presser at the clothing factory, was at work. When I asked if he could take me to his wife's sister, he stared blankly for a minute, then took me across to a small room at the eastern end of the north side of the courtyard. At the door he called out something which I did not quite catch. Then, seeing the door open, he pointed to me, saying "Someone to see you," and left.

The woman who opened the door appeared to be about fifty years of age; she was thin and frail and had a small oblong face with a pale, slightly sallow, complexion which, far from being coarse, was in fact quite delicate, but her forehead and the corners of her eyes and mouth were marked by tiny furrows. Her grey hair was drawn into a chignon, and from beneath her barely perceptible eyebrows a pair of large eyes stared in bewilderment, but this quickly changed to resignation, for she had been through all the vicissitudes which life has to offer. Having ushered me into the room, she looked me up and down and asked listlessly:

"Are you from the office?"

I told her who I was and why I had come. Watching me guarded-
ly, she seemed flustered and at a loss as to what she could do. In
order to alleviate the awkwardness of the situation, I tried first to
engage her in small talk, speaking in as warm and hearty a tone as
I could muster:

"Your husband's gone off to work?"

Her brow puckered and she replied stiffly:

"Him? He died ages ago, didn't he?"

It was only then I noticed that the room had just one single bed,
and that it was, moreover, far less orderly than the room from
which I had just come. The furniture consisted almost entirely of
inferior old pieces, with one possible exception — a high-legged
tea table of blackwood which stood beside the head of the bed. On
top of the table lay two objects, both of which were also far cleaner
and more eye-catching than anything else in the room: one was a
rather fancy cigarette lighter; the other, a fine porcelain lidded
bowl of quite classic elegance.

Still trying to smooth over my embarrassment, I asked casually:

"Your brother-in-law works out at the coal depot, doesn't he?"

For a moment she looked blank, then nodded, saying:

"You mean Qiuyun's husband? Yes, that's right. She works at the
clothing factory. I earn a little money at home pasting together
cardboard boxes." As she spoke, she pointed to a corner of the
room where I noticed piles of already assembled boxes and strips
of cardboard waiting to be pasted together.

Just as I was about to steer the conversation in the direction of
its main object — the recollection of the bitter past — the chairwoman of the Neighbourhood Committee suddenly appeared in
the doorway and said that she'd just had a call from the school.
Something urgent had come up, and I was to return immediately.
I had no alternative but to take my leave. Only when I reached the
lane did I discover that the chairwoman had played a trick on me.

This elderly lady now addressed me in a state of considerable agitation:

"It's not at all right for you to be asking that woman to recount her bitter past. Do you know who she is? She's the daughter of the Manchu prince whose mansion has now become your school. In the old days they used to call young ladies like that *Junjun* or sometimes *Duoluo Gege*, Manchu words for princess. After the Qing dynasty collapsed, over half of the mansion was sold to the foreign church, and they set up the school. The masters and mistresses of the mansion had to squeeze up in one of the side courtyards. They carried on in their decadent and dissolute way there, gradually eating up their fortune. After the Marco Polo Bridge Incident in 1937 the family sold the last remaining courtyard to the mission school, and that really was the end of them. The princess and her elder brother split up what the family still had left, then she moved into a courtyard house in Ram's-horn Lantern Lane — that was the last bit of property she had, and she made a living from renting out rooms. Just before Liberation, though, unbeknownst to her, her husband sold the house and took off with the proceeds. They'd been engaged as children by their parents. He was a bit of a fixer — in the old society he'd be out all day eating and drinking, going to brothels, gambling.... That was when she moved here, and up until the second year after Liberation she kept herself alive entirely by what she got from selling off her remaining paintings, calligraphy, antiques, porcelain, inkstones and that sort of thing. Eventually she got herself a bit of work to do at home, odd jobs really, separating sheets of mica, glueing boxes together, but at any rate she was supporting herself."

I was greatly startled, and inwardly cursed Uncle Shi. What did he think he was doing, telling me about a former aristocratic lady as if she were a member of the urban poor? At the same time I couldn't help asking:

"Is Qiuyun her younger sister?"

"She's no sister, she was her servant!" replied the old chairwoman.

"Qiuyun's never been able to raise the level of her class consciousness. She's so emotionally attached to the princess that she's incapable of drawing a class line between the two of them. The princess's name is Jin Qiwen. In all these years she's never stopped giving herself aristocratic airs. Even though she ended up so poor that she was washing her face and kneading her dough in the same enamel bowl, she never gave up two habits — smoking expensive cigarettes and drinking good tea. Before Liberation, Qiuyun stayed on with her to share her lonely life after her husband abandoned her, and ever since Liberation she's continued to look after her. In 1956 Qiuyun married Master Wang from the coal depot, but the two of them continued to treat Jin Qiwen well, completely ignoring the class barrier between them. Well, I ask you, however did you come up with the idea of getting a pair like that to tell the pupils about their bitter experiences?"

I was speechless, absolutely astounded. It had never occurred to me for an instant that people like this could still be living in the familiar streets and lanes round about. I'd never even read about them in the newspaper, in novels or in reports! Although they were living so close by, they seemed so utterly alien.

There now — I've got off the track. It's Uncle Shi we're supposed to be discussing; but to give a clear idea of him, it is necessary to say a bit about a few other people — and that brings me to the events of that decade of which, however much we might wish to forget it, we can never eradicate the memory.

IV

In particular, I shall never be able to forget the stifling summer of 1966, when our ordinary middle school was finally swept up by the political tornado.

I remember that morning, washing my face and getting into a water fight with Shuai, a teacher who shared my sleeping quarters. His full name was Shuai Tan, but, punning, we all used to call him Suan Tai, Garlic Shoot. We had heard about "the first Marxist-Leninist big-character poster" in an afternoon broadcast two days earlier. We had been amazed, puzzled, even curious, but we did not feel that it had anything to do with us personally. Then, as we walked out of the dormitory in the direction of the classroom building, we saw our own school's first big-character poster. The paste on the back of it was still hot and wet, and it was steaming around the edges of the paper. The poster was headed: "Party branch! Don't think you can get by under false pretences!" A crowd of teachers and pupils was gathered around it, their faces showing signs of great tension and confused emotions as they read it. The strange thing was that no one was actually discussing it or arguing about it.

The bell to commence classes rang. The first half of the first lesson went reasonably well, but then things fell apart. It began with wave after wave of cries from the exercise ground, and was shortly followed by the arrival of the first groups of student rebels, who came bursting into each and every classroom calling on everyone to assemble in the schoolyard. At the time I didn't have the faintest idea what was going on. The face of the rebel student who came charging into my classroom was twitching, and his blood seemed to be already well above boiling point. He made his appeal with such intense sincerity that I could see the tears glittering in his eyes. I cannot now remember exactly what it was that he cried out, but the gist of it was that revisionism had appeared within the Communist party: how could we sit quietly, attentively and respectably in our peaceful classroom, and not rush out to "sweep away all freaks and monsters"? After two minutes, the only people left in the classroom were a couple of the more timid pupils, together with myself — and even I, stunned as I was, found myself only a few minutes later walking over to the exercise ground.

It presented a scene of total chaos. A group of the most radical rebel students had surrounded Cao, who had only recently formally taken up the position of Party secretary. They were demanding that he admit to being a loyal associate of "the black municipal party committee", of "the black district party committee", and to practising revisionism. He didn't seem to be saying much, and some senior pupils together with a few of the younger teachers were bravely trying to defend him. One of them was Garlic Shoot, made very conspicuous by his tall and lanky figure, looking truly impassioned as he spoke, his face flecked with saliva.

By noon, two more big-character posters had appeared on either side of the first, one supporting it, the other launching a counter-attack. Garlic Shoot had written the latter, which called for the defence of the party committee, at great speed after returning to the dormitory. He had asked me to sign it, but I hesitated, asking him for a little more time to consider the matter, whereupon he had glared at me and stamped out of the dormitory to paste it up.

Towards dusk it was announced at great volume over the public address system that the Central Committee of the Communist Youth League had despatched a work group to the school, and that the party committee was to "stand to one side" and relinquish control. The leader of the working group clarified his position, coming out in support of the revolutionary students and the whole-hearted fashion in which they had thrown themselves into the movement. Once more Garlic Shoot set about writing another big-character poster in his dormitory, only this time he wrote slowly, working with furrowed brow. No sooner had he finished, however, than out he rushed to cover up his original poster with the new one, which proclaimed: "A warm welcome to the working group!" The opening sentence declared that "The deception practised on us by the party committee cannot go on forever …" He did not return to the dormitory for a long time that night, but instead raced off to the classroom of the upper third form, where the lights still burned brightly, in order to have a heart-to-heart discussion with rebel students and "to learn from the little generals".

For the next two or three days, ordinary run-of-the-mill people such as myself, with little experience of "movements", were at a complete loss. More and more big-character posters went up around the school until there was not an inch of space left on the wall of the toilet or on the wall round the exercise ground. The number of people mentioned and range of subjects covered by the posters also grew ever larger. Eventually there appeared a poster of no less than 17 sheets in length, entirely devoted to me. The main heading demanded that I be "unmasked", and the various subheadings were equally savage and to the point: "He propagates the black wares of feudalism, capitalism and revisionism"; "He instigates pupils to follow the 'white and expert' road"; "He viciously attacks the reform of Peking opera" and so on. Never before in my life had I seen myself attacked in a big-character poster, and my emotions were difficult to describe. Everything, it seemed, was finished. Life in this world was just too hard, too unjust — simply not worth living. What really stunned me was that amongst the "black words" of mine quoted in the poster were certain remarks which could only have been known to Garlic Shoot, things which I had said carelessly to him as we lay in our beds chatting after lights out.

That evening when I returned to the dormitory Garlic Shoot's face was sombre. He didn't speak to me, nor did he allow our eyes to meet; I realized he had already drawn a line between us. After a sleepless night I got up in the morning to discover that the soap had been taken from its dish on the rack where the face bowl was kept. It had been our practice to share my soap dish taking it in turns to buy the soap. This month's Green Treasure soap had been bought by Garlic Shoot, and now he had taken it away. This was a greater blow to me than his informing the "little generals" of the "black words" I had used in our chats. I suddenly felt weak, and sat down on the bed in a daze, almost in tears — how could a man change so drastically in just a few days?

After this, increasingly incomprehensible changes came thick and fast. At one moment the working group would declare the rebel pupils to be "rightists", "swimming fishes"; at another, the leader of the working group and Cao would be jointly subjected to a struggle session; the rebels themselves engaged in mutual expulsions and exposures; and finally Garlic Shoot moved out of the dormitory and set himself up with the "logistics section" of one particular faction of rebel pupils, where he became secretary to the little generals. Above the desk at which he daily scribbled away he hung a large portrait of Jiang Qing, Chairman Mao's wife.

Subsequent developments were increasingly violent. With "Red August" in 1966 the destruction of the Four Olds became universal, together with the launching of the "clean sweep" against class enemies. One afternoon the rebel "little generals" dragged a capitalist into the exercise ground, where he was alternately roughed up and struggled against, and after two hours beaten to death. Shortly before he died it had begun to thunder, and after his death the rain came. The "little generals" scattered all at once, leaving the exercise ground deserted. I sat in the dormitory, feeling a terrible weight on my heart. My mind was a blank, filled only by a feeling of physical revulsion. The realization that only a few dozen metres from my window lay a corpse, washed by the rain which grew heavier and heavier until it became a torrent, made me want to vomit.

The next morning I forced myself to go through the motions of washing, and set off for the classroom building to participate in the daily reading of Chairman Mao's quotations. Suddenly, I saw a sight which filled me with the most strange and conflicting emotions. What had I seen? To one side of the building, in the middle of a large puddle of water, stood Uncle Shi, his face expressionless, his trousers rolled up to reveal a pair of bandy legs, stubbornly trying to clear a blocked drainage pipe. In the background stood several scholar-trees, clean and glistening after the downpour. The wet leaves shone in the sunlight, while bright drops of water fell irregularly from their pointed tips, causing gentle ripples in the puddle in which the blue sky was reflected. Beneath the trees, several hollyhocks, which had for some reason escaped being uprooted by the heroes of the campaign to smash the Four Olds, still thrived, strong, wilful, brilliant, with clusters of pink flowers, large and small. This corner boasted no quotations, no big-character posters; it had instead a clean, quiet beauty. And Uncle Shi, as he worked away in this setting, seemingly having neither experienced nor witnessed the mad fury of the preceding days, appeared particularly pure and honest. I was startled at the tenacity with which he was clearing the drainage pipe of the fallen leaves and flowers which had blocked it, because at the time I — and I dare say the great majority of people — felt that life as it was now revealed before our eyes had lost its colour, its interest and its hope. If even the most precious cultural relics were to be smashed without pity, then what was the point of clearing a blocked pipe so that the accumulated water could drain away? What need was there for tidiness and cleanliness in a school where all order and discipline were anathema? As I dragged myself up the stairs I could not refrain from uttering a sigh of regret over Uncle Shi's insensitivity and obtuseness.

The atmosphere at the "daily reading" on that particular day was strange from the start. Garlic Shoot, responsible for the reading sessions of the teaching and research group, loudly led us in repeated recitations of the quotation beginning "After the enemies with guns have been wiped out, the enemies without guns will remain..." When the tension had reached the point where our very voices were quavering, he suddenly announced:

"In the small hours of this morning, a counter-revolutionary act was carried out in the grounds of our school. When the crematorium staff came to collect the body they discovered that the stinking corpse of that filthy capitalist swine, whose death was insufficient punishment for all his crimes, had actually been covered over with a sheet of plastic! This is not only a blatant act of support for the freaks and monsters, but also constitutes a frenzied counter-attack against the revolutionary little generals! We must drag out the counter-revolutionary activist responsible for laying on the plastic sheet! From now on, it is the duty of everyone to supply evidence which will enable us to prosecute and expose this counter-revolutionary. If he is in the room now, I hope he will reflect on the consequences of obstinate resistance!"

As he spoke, his eyes, which were rather refined, set in his handsome face, fixed each one of us in turn with a savage stare. I felt that he stared at me for an unusually long time.

Following the daily reading session, we would troop downstairs to peruse the big-character posters. Emerging from the building, we noticed a knot of people gathered in a circle, agitatedly looking at something. It was nothing other than the plastic sheet used by the "counter-revolutionary activist", which had been tied onto a rope and hoisted up for all to see in the hope that accusations would be made. As I edged forward to get a better look, my head was suddenly filled with a buzzing sound and my legs started to shake uncontrollably. My eyes could not possibly have deceived me, and I was the only teacher who could have recognized the fact: the plastic sheet was the one with which Uncle Shi normally covered his bed. At one end, it was marked with two holes caused by cigarette burns.

It took all the will-power at my command to conceal my feelings. When I finally got back to the dormitory and felt free to try to sort out in my own mind what all this meant, I kept coming back to the same questions: Why had Uncle Shi done it? What could he be thinking now? What would become of him were he to be found out? What would he do if misfortune befell him? How should I understand a person like him? How could the two actions of covering the corpse with the plastic sheet, and then going about the task of clearing the drain as if nothing had happened, be performed by one and the same Uncle Shi?

That afternoon, under the leadership of Garlic Shoot, the rebels began to inspect the sleeping quarters of all teachers and staff, paying particular attention to whether those whose beds were originally covered with plastic sheets still had them. I was in a continual state of anxiety over Uncle Shi, and did not dare to look in the direction of his room.

Towards evening, while the school loudspeaker was bellowing out: "We will certainly drag out the counter-revolutionary activist who lent flagrant support to the reactionary capitalist …", I looked out of the window and caught a glimpse of Uncle Shi, sweeping the path with his big bamboo broom. Instantly the apprehension which had been weighing on my heart fell away. I realized that Uncle Shi's room was probably the only place that Garlic Shoot and his gang had not bothered to check. As far as Garlic Shoot was concerned, Uncle Shi did not exist; nor was the little hut in which he lived, with its pine tree growing out of the roof tiles to quite a decent height, worthy of consideration as a dormitory.

I stayed by the window surreptitiously peeping out at Uncle Shi for a long time. Strange as it may seem, his face was, as always, quite without expression. It might have been carved in stone.

V

There were in fact so many "counter-revolutionary incidents" at that time that it was in practice quite impossible to get to the bottom of them all. After a period of hubbub, the "corpse-covering incident" simply faded away; and as it became ever less of an issue, my original attitude of concern for Uncle Shi gradually turned to one of resentment of his stupidity. Why should he, a member of the "five red elements", put himself at risk for the sake of a capitalist, an exploiter? He was dead anyway, so why bother? What sort of class feeling was this! I had almost concluded that Uncle Shi was a fool, with neither class feeling nor a head for politics, when something happened to make me change my mind.

The occasion was a mass criticism and struggle meeting against the "capitalist roader" Cao, called jointly by the two main rebel organizations. Before the meeting I had already learned that Garlic Shoot had specially sought out Uncle Shi in order to mobilize him for the struggle. In the first half of 1966 the Education Bureau had demanded that the school arrange to have a number of male staff aged 55, and female staff aged 50, take early retirement in order to bring in new blood without exceeding staff ceilings. At the time, Uncle Shi was already 55, but there was some dispute within the school leadership over the question of his retirement. One opinion had it that he would certainly have to go in order to make way for a new member of staff. Cao, however, would not agree to this, maintaining that as Uncle Shi was a single man, the school had become his home. Even if he formally retired, he would still continue to sweep and clean as he had done for decades; but after retirement his monthly income would drop by forty percent. It was low enough already, and he would have even greater difficulty supporting himself. Finally, the two sides agreed on a compromise: Uncle Shi would formally retire, but the Education Bureau would be petitioned to continue to pay his original salary. After a great deal of effort on Cao's part, this plan was finally implemented. Now, Garlic Shoot and his group told Uncle Shi that what Cao had done was "corrupting the working class through economism" in order to "buy over people's hearts, numb their resolve to struggle, and frenziedly carry out the revisionist line in education". Apparently, while Garlic Shoot and company were priming Uncle Shi to make a statement at Cao's criticism and struggle session, he had not said a word, his face maintaining its wonted blank expression. Garlic Shoot explained repeatedly to Shi that if he made an accusation he would not as a result get a forty-percent salary reduction the following month — he would be paid his full salary.

"We're not doing this for the money, but to criticize the capitalist roaders, right?"

In the face of such reiterated assurances and declarations, Uncle Shi finally nodded his assent.

"All right. I'll say a few words."

The scale of the criticism and struggle meeting was comparatively large because "everyone is responsible for criticizing the revisionist line in education", so residents from the neighbourhood were also brought in to participate. The "capitalist-roader ruffians" were lined up on the two sides of the rostrum in goose-wing formation, and each of these lesser targets of the struggle session was forced to bow low and hang a placard around his neck. Cao, who had been marched to the centre of the rostrum, had a weight from the heaviest dumb-bell hung from his neck. Although Uncle Shi's statement was not included amongst the "heavy guns" deployed by Garlic Shoot and his friends, the latter nevertheless had a particular motive in having him make it:

namely, to let the "revolutionary masses" in the audience realize that as even someone like Shi Yihai had come forward to make an accusation, they could obviously have no further reservations about confirming Cao as a capitalist roader.

Garlic Shoot announced in his shrill voice: "Comrade Shi Yihai will now make his accusation", and from the crowd below, as I watched Uncle Shi, seemingly impervious to feeling, stride up with his bandy legs onto the rostrum, I felt as if my heart was being torn to shreds. I was filled with an indescribable sadness.

Uncle Shi walked up to the microphone, his face still devoid of any obvious emotion, and began to speak in a normal conversational tone.

"The Communist Party's never treated me badly." No sooner had he uttered this sentence than those both on the rostrum and in the audience realized that something rather unusual was happening, particularly as having delivered this statement he gave the masses in the audience further cause for surprise by turning to face Cao, who was almost fainting under the weight of the great iron disc. The scene which immediately followed shook the entire assembly. Making his way steadily across the rostrum to Cao, before the intent gaze of all present, Uncle Shi took the weight from around his neck, then turned back to Garlic Shoot and the other accusers and asked, still in a perfectly even tone:

"What did the Communist Party ever do wrong to you that you have to use such a harsh punishment?"

He then bent down and gently placed the weight on the rostrum floor and confidently strode back down into the crowd of onlookers.

At first all were hushed. Not even a cough could be heard. Then there came a murmur, which quickly rose in volume, and commotion broke out. Up on the rostrum, the rebel leaders responsible for holding the meeting were furious, but seemed divided as to

what to do. It was obvious that some of them wished to seize Uncle
Shi immediately and drag him up onto the rostrum to join those
being struggled against, but others felt that to do this would not
necessarily be to their advantage. In the end it was Garlic Shoot
who showed the readiest wit. He rushed across to the microphone
and grasping it firmly in his hand announced:

"This action of Shi Yihai's must be... discussed later! It shows
how deeply he has been corrupted by those who wish to preserve
the old dispensation! We hope that Shi Yihai will realize his mistake before he has gone too far. If he persists in his reactionary
stand, he will be responsible for all the consequences. Don't let it
be said that he hasn't been warned!"

By the time Garlic Shoot got to his final sentence, however,
Uncle Shi had already returned to his little hut in the corner of the
exercise ground and shut the door.

Garlic Shoot was just about to call upon the next speaker when
from the edge of the crowd there came a weak but shrill and
desolate cry. Then somebody stood up, and supporting another
person, left the meeting site. An elderly lady had been so fright-
ened by the scene which we had just witnessed that she had fainted
(perhaps she had also been affected by the hot sun beating down
on her head for such a long time). In the brief instant in which I
saw her being carried away I realized that she was none other than
Jin Qiwen, whom I had met only once before; and surely the
person supporting her was Qiuyun? The man who followed on
behind them was without question Master Wang from the coal
depot.

I do not wish to pursue my account of the criticism and struggle
meeting any further. Uncle Shi was fortunate. Before Garlic Shoot
and company had a chance to take their revenge against him, they
were themselves caught up in the dramatically changing situation
at the school. At one moment one faction seized power, at the

next, another. Then the faction in power would split in two. When the first Mao Zedong Thought Workers' Propaganda Team entered the school, all the factions lost power — until the second such propaganda team arrived to announce that the first team had been mistaken in its general line. Somehow or other it came to pass that Garlic Shoot himself eventually joined the ranks of those on the rostrum being struggled against: he was accused of being a member of the "16 May counter-revolutionary conspiracy". When I saw him in obvious pain being forced into the "aeroplane position", head down and arms stretched out behind him, I pitied him — but not too much.

The high point of all these dramatic events occurred on the day when the Mao Zedong Thought Workers' Propaganda Team held a "Leniency and Severity Mass Meeting". As Garlic Shoot had confessed his crimes with a good attitude, he was treated with leniency in accordance with the doctrine of letting bygones be bygones. There was, however, another person who had been exposed on account of his evidence. The evidence having been checked by a group set up specially to examine the case, this person was to be immediately subjected to the most severe punishment. Just as I was trying to guess who this person could possibly be, a great cry suddenly filled my ears — the order to drag me up onto the rostrum! What a joke — the "carefully concealed key member of the 16 May Group" was none other than myself!

Under circumstances such as these, the last thing I needed to worry about was what sort of a person Uncle Shi was. Unless, that is, I were to take a leaf from Garlic Shoot's book and expose Shi as a core element of the 16 May plotters!

VI

It is said that small temples house powerful gods, and shallow ponds harbour many turtles. Thus it was that during the "purifying class ranks" movement, no less than twenty-one teachers and staff, a little over 19.3 per cent of the total of our small middle school, were subjected to the "dictatorship of the proletariat". Apart from writing self-criticisms and being subjected to struggle and criticism, we were also made to undergo reform through labour. The heaviest task was digging up the roots of trees. For some reason unknown to me, five scholar-trees had been felled in the nearby Bamboo Leaf Lane, so together with nine other reactionary "cow-spirits", I was given the duty of excavating their deeply rooted stumps. One of those assigned to my group, which had been ordered to remove the largest stump at the far end of the alley, was Uncle Ge from the reception office, whom I have already mentioned.

On the first day we hardly exchanged a word, simply occupying ourselves with our labours. This was not because we were working under supervision, but because we were not sure of one another. The crime for which Uncle Ge was being punished was that of being a "core member of a reactionary Taoist secret society"; just as he did not know whether or not I was really a member of the mysterious 16 May organization, so too I could not be sure whether or not this former Taoist priest (albeit a married man) really deserved retribution for a life filled with evil. But after all we were human beings, social animals, so it was not possible for the two of us to continue to ignore one another forever, finding satisfaction in our own individual loneliness and silence. On the second day of continuous labour on the stump, once the rest-break came around we could no longer resist the impulse to speak.

I addressed Uncle Ge quite frankly.

"Calling me a '16 May element' is a complete farce. The principal piece of evidence they came up with was the fact that I'd once written a letter to Xiao Hua. Now they're saying that Xiao Hua was an influential backer of the 16 May Group, so that's supposed to make me a leading member. Actually the letter I wrote to him was entirely devoted to a discussion of rhyme and rhythm in his 'Long March Song Cycle'."

Uncle Ge was squatting on the ground opposite me, his thin bony torso covered only by a singlet. His dry, wrinkled skin, flecked with liver spots, was soaked with sweat, and the veins in his long skinny arms stood out alarmingly like the bluish bodies of dead worms. Seeing that I was no longer treating him as an outsider, he spoke to me quite earnestly:

"When I was a child, I lived in a Taoist temple as a priest. Later on after the temple's property was all squandered and the chief priest kicked the bucket, I left with four others who were junior to me, and we made our living performing funeral rites, prayers for the dead and other such nonsense whenever we came across a wealthy family where there'd been a death. If you're talking about preaching superstition, sucking up to the rich and that sort of thing, sure, I've done it, and I ought to be punished for whatever I've done wrong. But I can't for the life of me accept that I deserve a hundred deaths for my hatred of the new society."

We looked at each other, and from the sincerity in one another's eyes we realized that there was no further need for "internal and external investigations", as was the fashion of the time. The look that we exchanged created sympathy and trust, and from then on we were more considerate of one another and co-ordinated our efforts as we wielded our picks around the stump.

It was a really burning summer. Hot sweat used to seep continually from our skin like water through a muslin cloth, and the sweat stains on our shirts accumulated layer after layer. The school, however, did not provide us with water, so when we were thirsty we had to go to a nearby courtyard and take our fill of cold water from the tap. To me it was like the purest rainwater, but it made life quite impossible for Uncle Ge and some of the other "cow-spirits" who suffered from stomach complaints. This was especially so in the case of Ge, who had a very bad ulcer: if he didn't drink, he felt as if he were carrying a lump of burning coal in his belly; but if he drank unboiled tap-water, the sensation was that of shards of ice tumbling into his stomach. It was really painful to watch him with his cheeks sucked in, his dry lips pressed tightly together, his prominent Adam's apple moving up and down in spasms as he sought to control his raging thirst.

On the afternoon of the second day, as the waves of heat beat down with a truly manic intensity, I suddenly caught sight of Uncle Shi, a serious expression fixed on his face, coming towards us trundling a handcart from the inside of which protruded a pick-axe.

"Look! He's been caught too!" I said, pointing him out to Uncle Ge.

"I knew he wouldn't be able to escape", replied Ge, lowering his head painfully as he added: "He hardly ever says a thing, but when he does, well… he says enough to have himself condemned as counter-revolutionary activist right away."

Uncle Shi stopped his cart just in front of the hole which we had dug around the stump. Only then did I notice that the handcart also contained a bucket covered with a damp cloth. As he raised the cloth, our nostrils were assailed by the steaming aroma of mung bean soup. Before Ge and I had recovered from our speech-less amazement, Uncle Shi had already ladled out an enamel bowl full of the green liquid, which he handed to Ge, saying in a perfectly normal tone:

"Drink up. If that's not enough you can have some more."

As Uncle Ge lifted his head to drain the bowl, I could see that not only did the warm soup trickle from the corners of his mouth, but his eyes were filled with moisture too.

We soon learned that Uncle Shi had not in fact been "dragged out", nor had he been ordered to bring us liquid refreshment. The beans were his, and he had cooked them on his own stove for us. I noted with amazement that he dispensed the soup to all without exception, even to a "counter-revolutionary activist", a man with a genuine criminal record who had maliciously attacked Chairman Mao and the Party and whom not even I nor Uncle Ge could forgive. One bowl was not enough for him, but he seemed to be afraid to ask for a second and shrank back licking his lips, where-upon Uncle Shi, without a moment's hesitation, ladled out another bowlful and handed it to him.

Even more surprisingly, once he'd finished dishing out the soup Uncle Shi picked up his pickaxe and set about helping everyone in turn with their respective tree stumps. When he got to us, he motioned to Uncle Ge to go and take a rest by the wall, then raised his pick and together we attacked the stubborn stump. I couldn't help asking:

"Uncle Shi, won't you get into trouble doing this?"

Putting down his pick, he fixed me with his gaze and replied:

"It's all right. If you lot aren't old or sick then you're scholars — I ought to give you a hand."

In my heart I was grateful, but nevertheless felt that the matter should still be looked at according to the dialectical principle of "one divides into two", so motioning with my mouth in the direction of the counter-revolutionary activist, I said:

"But he really did launch vicious attacks against the Great Leader, so you certainly shouldn't help him."

To my surprise, Uncle Shi replied without hesitation:

"He's guilty and should be punished — but he should still be treated decently. The more you treat him like a human being, the quicker he's likely to mend his ways."

I was stunned.

The third day was overcast, and Uncle Shi didn't come. During our break, Uncle Ge and I got to talking about him. Ge nodded his head in agreement when I commented on what a strange person Shi was. He looked around, and then, lowering his voice he began to speak, his deeply sunken cheeks twitching every few seconds.

"Old Shi certainly is a bit of a puzzle. There's something I've been keeping to myself all this while and haven't dared to mention openly before. Still, seeing as you too believe he's a good fellow and won't blow the whistle on him and suck up to 'them', I'll tell you. You remember when they were destroying the Four Olds, how the Red Guards reckoned I was a member of the working class? Well, because of that they used to put all the stuff they'd taken from houses that they'd ransacked in the neighbourhood into the empty room next to the reception office, and gave me the job of keeping an eye on it at night. Of course they stuck a dirty great padlock on the door and kept the key. Well, I remember on one rainy night, around midnight, I heard someone tapping softly on the office door. I opened the door to see who it was, and lo and behold, it was Shi! 'What's up?' I asked him. 'What are you up to in the middle of the night like this?' 'Ge,' he asked, 'did they do over Bamboo Leaf Lane today?' 'You bet they did,' I replied. 'They got even more this time than before, the room's nearly full up!' While I was talking I was looking at him, and I had a feeling something queer was going on. After all, Shi didn't have any friends or relations there, so why should he bother about Bamboo Leaf Lane? Why was he asking? I certainly couldn't tell what he was really on about from looking at his face. For several minutes he just stood there with his mouth shut. Then, suddenly, he came straight to the point. 'Open up the middle door and let me in to have a look.' Just to hear him say such a thing scared me out of my wits. It's true that there is a door connecting the reception office to the storeroom next to it, but it had been sealed up with a wooden plank years ago. My voice was trembling as I said to him, 'You might be tired of living, but you don't have to get others involved too!' When he saw the state I was in, he didn't say anything more but just walked up to the door and removed the plank with a few twists of the pliers that he'd brought for the purpose, opened the door and went into the storeroom. I hurried in behind him, not knowing rightly what I ought to do — I felt as if I had hundreds of centipedes crawling all over me.

"The first thing he looked at when he went in was the furniture. I kept my eyes fixed on him, and saw his eyes suddenly light up as he caught sight of one particular piece. Grabbing it with his great hands, he said to himself out loud, 'So they really took this too.' It was a tea table, carved out of hardwood. As far as I could see, there was nothing particularly special about it. After all, there was any amount of good furniture that had been confiscated. Then he started going very carefully through the antiques that had all been piled up in a heap. Piece by piece he looked at them, then put them to one side. By the time he'd finished, his whole head was covered with drops of sweat the size of soya beans, but from the really funny look that he had in his eyes he seemed to be especially pleased about something. He didn't take a thing, simply walked out of the storeroom and then sealed it up again just like it was before. He thanked me, then disappeared in the blink of an eye. He'd put me in such a state that I didn't dare to go to sleep, and the next morning my heart started thumping like a drum whenever I saw anybody. But the Red Guards never did find out about it — I suppose Shi'd just got Lady Luck on his side and wasn't fated to be caught."

The immediate effect of hearing Ge's story was to increase even further the aura of mystery surrounding Uncle Shi. What sort of a man was he? It seemed that to really understand what made him tick, it was pointless trying to rely on quotations from the Chairman, searching the files, class analyses, internal investigations and external assignments, the policy of leniency to those who come clean and severity to those who resist, or giving credit to forced confessions. Previously I'd believed that Uncle Shi was a very simple and backward type not worth bothering about, a character of no interest whatsoever. But now it seemed that in a world gone mad, where chaos and the extraordinary ruled the day, he alone was able to remain true to himself and resist being swept this way and that by the fierce and angry tides.

After almost thirty hours of strenuous labour spread over three days, we eventually succeeded in uprooting the octopus-like tree stump. As we were wheeling our handcarts back to the school, carrying the remnants of the stump, overcome with exhaustion as I was I allowed my cart to topple over halfway down the lane, spilling mud and pieces of stump in all directions. Uncle Ge helped me to right the cart, and then bent down and started to pick up the mess.

"Forget it, somebody sweeps the lane anyhow," I said to him. Sweat glistened from his temples as he continued to clean up the dirt and splintered wood, saying with a sigh:

"The person whose punishment it is to sweep this alley is the former princess. She's well over fifty now, and in very poor health, so we ought to do what we can to help her save her strength."

The image of Jin Qiwen appeared in my mind, but it gave rise to no feeling of sympathy, and I replied, unmoved:

"Well her health can't be too bad, can it? After all, she's able to sweep a long alley like this every day."

Uncle Ge stood up, placed his sinewy hands on the side of the cart, and though he was panting, said softly:

"I've heard say that every night after midnight someone does it for her, and only leaves the last thirty yards or so for her to finish off in the first light of dawn — otherwise she'd have been coughing blood and kicked the bucket ages ago!"

This really set me back, but just at that moment Master Wang appeared, his face covered with coal dust, riding towards us on a pedal cart laden with honey-comb coal briquettes. I recalled the mindless loyalty shown towards Jin Qiwen by Wang and Qiuyun, and began to understand. I didn't say any more, and continued on my way back to the school, pushing my handcart.

VII

Another hot and sticky summer. On the day of which I now write, the school grounds appeared unusually clean and beautiful. The initial impression was of a ship which after having battled the raging seas bore the survivors of the storm into a tranquil harbour.

The morning sun lent added lustre to the red paint on the plaque over the school gate bearing the quotation from Chairman Mao, while the golden Chinese characters shone with unwonted brilliance. Beneath the archway potted flowers had been arranged in two curving lines: long green fronds trailed down from the asparagus bamboo, while small bell-like buds hung from the red-cluster flowers. Even the archway had been decorated on both sides by a palm-tree growing in a tub. Surprise, however, was uncalled for. To understand all, it was only necessary to walk a little way up the path leading to the main school building, where the colourfully adorned blackboard stood. A bunch of roses in full bloom had been drawn on the board with coloured chalk, across which was written in English and Chinese the following exhortation: "Warmly welcome the visit to our school by the foreign guest from X!"

It was already 1973. The workers' propaganda team had by now changed leaders several times, but whoever it was without exception simultaneously filled the position of secretary of the school

Party branch. Cao, who had eventually been "liberated", had become deputy secretary. Following the thaw in Sino-US relations in 1972, foreigners started visiting China once again, and, moreover, where six years previously they might at any time have been seized and insulted by Red Guards, now the situation was so changed that wherever they went they were invested with magic powers which caused the appearance of the place visited to undergo a transformation.

At about 7:30 in the morning a debate was initiated amongst the three people in the rather resplendently appointed "reception room". And who were these three? One was Cao. He was dressed in ordinary clothes, with his dark and solid neck emerging from his open collar. His thick eye-brows were slightly drooping, an indication that he was not in the best of spirits. He was critical of the hypocrisy of the arrangements that had been made in order to receive this single foreign guest. The sofa, tea-table, carpet, drawn silk curtains and other such props had all been brought over from the district office in order to create this reception room. What was more, the "flowers for political use" — the palms, the asparagus bamboo, the red-clusters, had all been borrowed for the occasion from the nearby park. The classroom to be visited had been newly whitewashed, the broken windows repaired, the old wooden blackboard replaced by one of fibreglass, and the best chairs in the school gathered together there. Even the pupils in attendance had been selected from each form on the basis of a triple examination of their political suitability, appearance and aptitude displayed in an oral test. The girls, moreover, had to wear floral print dresses. This created considerable difficulty for the parents of those selected to take part in these "diplomatic activities", as whatever dresses might originally have been owned had long ago been put to other uses following the destruction of the Four Olds, so material had to be bought and new ones run up. All these things taken together had resulted in Cao's being overcome by a feeling of revulsion about the whole business. However, at that time the real boss of the school was the leader of the workers' propaganda team, Fan. He would be arriving at the school around eight o'clock, dressed in his "reception outfit", to perform his role as the responsible person receiving the honoured foreign visitor against the backdrop so carefully prepared by the rest of us. It was his wont never to allow himself to be contaminated by the slightest practical consideration, but if anything were to go wrong in the course of the proceedings it would be us — especially Cao — who would have to take the blame.

Standing opposite Cao was Garlic Shoot, got up in his own brand new reception rig: dark grey jacket of "three-in-one" blended fabric, sharply creased trousers of black stretched dacron, and black leather shoes shining like mirrors. Following the decision of the workers' propaganda team to treat him leniently, and after repeated re-education sessions at the team office, he had now long since attained that happy and harmonious state whereby he could spend the entire night seated around the card table with team leader Fan and his associates. Fan had appointed him a member of the reception group, and it was as a result of his tireless efforts that the various arrangements made on orders from above had been put into place. Happy now, but still not completely satisfied, worried that there might still be some flaw which would not become apparent until the visit was already underway, he had suddenly thought to warn Uncle Shi to keep out of the way while the foreigner was present. "Of course", he was saying, "we can just tell Uncle Shi to his face that it's to avoid his being stumped for an answer if the foreigner asks him a question. What really worries me, though, is the way he looks — those bandy legs …"

White with anger, the veins on his neck strained to bursting, Cao interrupted, "So what about bandy legs? Uncle Shi is a fine and

genuine Chinese — how do you justify a Chinese in his own country hiding from a foreigner?"

Standing to one side, I too was shaking with rage. I had also
been "liberated" not long after the 13 September Incident,[1] and
had already returned to my teaching position. I was, moreover, the
best foreign language teacher in the school, so it had been arranged that the foreign guest should observe my language class. I
was also dressed in my best clothes, but like Cao I was revolted by
the falsity of the proceedings. Even so, it had never occurred to me
that Garlic Shoot would go so far as to order Uncle Shi to stay out
of sight. That was really going too far! Taking up Cao's point, I
declared, "Uncle Shi's bandy legs are the result of imperialist
oppression, they're nothing that the Chinese people should be
ashamed of. What's more, through all the ups and downs of the
last few years I reckon that he's never done a thing to hurt anyone.
He's a damn sight more beautiful — spiritually and physically —
than some people I could mention!"

Seeing that Cao and I were genuinely angry, Garlic Shoot suddenly broke into a smile and, his face all innocence, reproached
himself:

"Forget it, forget it, it's just me being a busy-body... actually by
the time the foreign guest gets here Uncle Shi will have finished
sweeping the grounds and gone back to his room anyway, so
there's no way in which they'd come across each other...."

Garlic Shoot was like that — he had the knack of winning your
forgiveness with his totally innocent expression just when you were
really furious with him. I remember how he was when Cao was
restored to his original position: he neither wept tears of remorse

---

[1]   This refers to Lin Biao's failed coup d'etat and his death, reportedly in an
aeroplane crash, in 1971.

nor showed any evidence of shame, but simply walked up to him, shrugged his shoulders, and with a tone and expression so innocent as to appear positively naive, he simply said, "When I struggled against you in the past I was mistaken — I was had, taken in! But in a movement on a scale like that, I'm sure you're not going to hold my little mistake against me!" What could Cao say? Of course he replied, "It doesn't really matter."

Anyhow, repressing my feelings of vexation and resentment, I made the best of a bad job and together with group leader Fan, Garlic Shoot and the others, I managed to fulfill my "reception duty". Actually the foreign guest was just a young chap, not much more than twenty. He'd come to China as a member of a tourist group, and had requested that he be allowed to visit a university and a high school in order to gain an understanding of the achievements of China's "revolution in education", which was to be the subject of an article he intended to write when he returned home. Before coming to China he had already undertaken to supply a certain magazine with articles of this sort. Quite contrary to the expectations of the spruced up and highly polished Fan and Garlic Shoot, the foreign guest had closely cropped hair and wore Chinese-style blue cotton pants and jacket; he was shod in a pair of sandshoes. What was more, he admitted to having suffered from polio, and there was something not right about his legs, which looked bandy to me, although in his case they were bent inwards, making him knock-kneed. He was completely taken in by us, and kept nodding his head and uttering words of praise. How could he know that so many of the fine things on display had been put on show just for the occasion? When the time came for him to take his leave he was obviously much moved, and with tears in his eyes he firmly grasped group leader Fan by the hand, saying, "The Cultural Revolution is good! The revolution in education is good! When I get home I'll certainly write an article to refute the insulting and slanderous accusations that China has destroyed education!" The interpreter too seemed in the grip of considerable emotion as he put the words into Chinese and group leader Fan's face was shining — you could see he really was filled with genuine gratitude and great happiness. Garlic Shoot was grinning so broadly that his eyes were reduced to two narrow slits. As I looked at the young foreigner I was thinking, if only what you've seen were real ...

No sooner had our excursion into international diplomacy ended than Garlic Shoot got busy ordering people to remove the palms, take away the potted flowers, and generally restore everything to its original condition lest the teachers and pupils be stricken by such poisonous influences. Unable to find an outlet for my repressed sense of wrong and frustration, I decided I might as well take myself off to Uncle Shi's room. Opening the door, I looked in and saw Cao sitting opposite him. They were both smoking, and their feet were surrounded by the butts of the cigarettes they had been rolling themselves from leaf tobacco. For the first time in my life I stretched out my hand and said "Roll one for me."

After this, whenever I felt depression coming on, off I'd go to Uncle Shi's room. At the beginning he didn't say much — it was mainly him listening to me pour my heart out. One of the greatest blessings in life must surely be the ability to give full vent to one's innermost feelings in the presence of another person, without the slightest need to protect oneself. I spoke to him about the death of Uncle Ge, who had not survived until the 13 September Incident, but died under the "dictatorship of the proletariat". He had left behind him his wife, whose job it was to keep an eye on the bicycles parked in front of the department store, and a daughter who had been sent down to a village in the countryside. With his death their lives must have become even more difficult.

"Perhaps," I said, "Uncle Ge really did commit some evil acts in the past, but from my personal knowledge of him I felt that he was a good man."

Calmly, Uncle Shi replied, "Yes, we're none of us saints. As long as you don't set out to hurt someone deliberately, then you're a good man."

Gradually I began to ask him questions.

"Do you believe in God?"

I knew that he'd been in the service of foreign priests since he was a child, so he was sure to have been converted. To my surprise he replied frankly, "I can't really say I believe, because I've never seen him. I only believe in things I've seen with my own eyes."

I challenged this.

"The human eye is limited in what it can see. Take magnetism, for instance, or electric current, or things on the other side of a wall — you can't see them with your naked eye. Sometimes for psychological reasons your eyes can deceive you and you'll halluci-nate, like that ghost girl you told me about before. Now that must have been a hallucination."

He thought a little, then said, "Perhaps there are times when your eyes deceive you. But people shouldn't lie about what they haven't seen — that's what I call going against your conscience."

The more I thought about it the more I became aware of the depth of his words, which on first hearing had seemed so common-place. This led me to think of what he had said when we were all digging up tree stumps the previous summer, and I realized that Uncle Shi must have his own philosophy of life. Finally unable to restrain myself any longer, I asked him, "When the students beat that capitalist to death during the campaign against the Four Olds, it was you who covered him with a plastic sheet. I recognized the sheet as yours, but of course up till now I haven't breathed a word to anyone. Still, I don't understand — how could someone coming from such a harsh background as yours have pity on a capitalist?"

He fixed his gaze on me, and throwing away the cigarette butt that he'd had in his hand he replied ingenuously, "That man they killed was called Sun, his family used to run a grocery here in the neighbourhood before Liberation. Nobody liked him, he was famous for his stinginess — in fact he was such a miser that when someone in his family trimmed their fingernails he'd gather up the pieces in a sheet of newspaper and take them off to sell to the medicine shop! But he wasn't guilty of any capital crime! So even though he did meet with disaster and ended up being beaten to death, it wasn't right just to leave his body out there soaking in the rain. He was a human being too. There are limits that should not be crossed in the way people treat each other. Why did I respect the Communist Party at the time of Liberation? Because I reckoned that they didn't degrade people. They arrested gangsters, local bullies, and got rid of them for the sake of the people, one bullet and that was it; they didn't treat them like a cat with a mouse, playing games with it first, not eating it until it's almost torn to pieces. I just don't know what's happened over the last few years, people doing each other over, trampling on one another, it's become all the rage. Whenever we have a criticism and struggle meeting at the school, somebody gets dragged out, they hang a placard round his neck, stick a tall hat on his head, poke him and grab him, shave half his hair off, make him sing the 'Howling Song' or whatever it's called. It's just not right, I reckon. To tell you the truth, even if the person really was a wrong'un, you treat him like that and I'd end up feeling sorry for him, just as you'd feel sorry for anyone who's not treated as a human being by other people. You lot are always going on about class struggle; well, class struggle means people struggling against each other, it doesn't mean people struggling against dogs, does it? So there ought to be limits, things shouldn't be allowed to take on the inhuman form they've taken now...."

Emerging from Uncle Shi's little room with its odour of old bedding and cheap tobacco, I was reluctant to return to my own dormitory straight away, and instead walked for a long time along the path around the exercise ground. Gazing up at the Milky Way, twinkling so gently in the night sky, I was repeatedly overcome by an unaccountable emotion. The simple yet deep words that I have just quoted struck me like a deafening thunder-clap of enlightenment in the midst of those cheerless, chaotic and difficult years.

As time went by I found it increasingly difficult to get through the evenings without visiting Uncle Shi's little room, and I sensed that his feelings towards me had grown as had mine towards him. There was one particularly hot evening, so hot that even the leaves on the trees seemed to be panting for breath, and the cicadas continued their noisy chorus long after the sun had set. The air felt like the breath of a blast furnace. When I went to Uncle Shi's room I discovered to my surprise that Master Wang from the coal depot was sitting opposite him, and from their appearance the two men appeared to have been deep in conversation for quite some time.

Both Uncle Shi and Master Wang were stripped to the waist because of the heat. I was amazed to see what a powerful torso Uncle Shi had. He was already over sixty, at the very least older than Master Wang by two or three years, but while the latter was certainly solidly built, his prominent muscles were beginning to show signs of flabbiness. The muscles on Uncle Shi's barrel chest, on the other hand, were still taut and firm. Although an unfortunate childhood had deformed his legs, long years of labour had nevertheless given him an upper body that was strong and handsome. The two men were seated cross-legged on the bed-cover, and on the low *kang*-table between them there was an empty liquor bottle and a similarly depleted plate. The room was full of the smell of spirits. A rosy afterglow of alcohol suffused Master Wang's broad face. Coal dust seemed actually to have grown into the flesh of his deeply lined cheeks, and this made him look rather like one of those fierce warriors from an old romance. Uncle Shi's face was also slightly flushed over his cheek-bones and, something that was very rare for him, his eyes were shining. No sooner had I arrived than Master Wang draped his shirt over his shoulders, got down from the bed and took his leave. Uncle Shi made no attempt to detain him. I sat down where he had been sitting, but as I've never been able to sit cross-legged I just perched on the edge of the bed.

Looking at me, Uncle Shi made a suggestion:

"Don't go back to your room tonight. There's something I need to discuss with you, so we may as well stay up talking till morning."

I felt both honoured and surprised. Up until then I had always been the one who initiated the conversation, and his principal role had been that of listener and respondent. What, then, could be special about this evening?

That night I had an experience which I shall never forget as long as I live.

VIII

Imagine an old, deserted garden.

The darkened lacquer on the pavilion is already flaking away in places, and the tiny dried-up pond resembles an eye covered with a cataract. Half of the stone balustrade on the small bridge across it has fallen down, and moss grows thickly around the sides of the well. Some of the trees in the garden are dead but have not been cut down, their sinister branches starting upwards into the clear sky, while others in the arbour have grown crazily and knotted themselves together with the untended shrubs that have run wild beneath them, blocking the pathways which formerly ran there. Rushes and weeds have grown up over the steps, and small trees emerging from the cracks between the stone slabs which originally served to pave the bridge and steps have pushed them up into crazy angles. Insects of every kind scuttle in and out of the shady corners, birds have built their nests in the trees and reed clumps, and the columns of the arcade, the railings and the stone steps are covered with their grey-white droppings. A gust of autumn wind brings forth a rustling sound from all about, accompanied by the cawing of a crow.

It is almost noon on an early autumn day, and a grotesque scene presents itself beside the well: a young manservant, aged about seventeen or eighteen, his two hands fastened behind his back with a rope, one arm drawn back over his shoulder, the other pulled up diagonally across his back to meet it, is ceaselessly treading a mass of yellow clay beneath his feet. He is none other than the youthful Shi Yihai.

At the time of the scene we have just described, the ruined garden was still the property of the prince, but the foreign priests were in the midst of negotiations with his steward to buy it. In fact, the gourd-shaped gateway connecting the garden to the church school, occupied by the priests, had been opened up long since, and Father Ai'er, without bothering about the fact that the negotiations for its purchase had not yet been concluded, looked on the garden as his own. Having heard that the yellow clay there was of the type considered most suitable for making clay figurines, he had already hired a master of the art from Tianjin. He planned to have him create a series of figurines which he could take back to Europe as gifts for his relatives and friends when he went home for consultations with his superiors at the beginning of winter. In order to increase the viscosity of the excavated clay, he had ordered Shi Yihai to spend an entire day treading it underfoot. Given the fact that Shi was generally none too obedient, when he was taken into the garden the priest had had him tied up in the fashion described, his two thumbs fastened firmly together with a bootlace.

This painful position was known as "Su Qin carrying his sword".

No punishment caused Shi Yihai greater agony than this. It was not so much the pain — whippings and kicks from booted feet hurt far worse — as the humiliation. In this position he felt he was not human, not even a beast, but simply a toy to be battered at will by whoever wished to do so, a mouse fallen into the clutches of a cat. The early autumn sun was as hot as it had ever been in summer, and within a very short time Shi Yihai was drenched with sweat. Although he was only a few feet from the well, he was unable to use his hands to get himself any water. He wished he could tear out of the ruined garden and hurl himself at Father Ai'er, even at the risk of his life, but he knew that no good would come of it if he did; the other priest, Father De Taibai, the one he thought of as a good and just man, was out of town, and there was nobody who could protect him. Thoughts of flight also filled his mind, but even if he were able to get away from the garden, people seeing him trussed up as he was would immediately realize that he was a fugitive miscreant. He wanted to resist but was unable to do so, and his legs, impelled by a sort of inertia, mechanically trampled the dampened clay. It wasn't very long before they became numb.

Though he had lost track of time, he became aware of the sound of a woman's sobbing, which came to him wave after wave until it occupied his entire attention. Was it the Blessed Virgin who had descended to earth, or was it some all too human damsel in distress? Looking all about him, he finally identified the sound as coming from the direction of the western chamber, where thorn bushes had already grown as high as the window ledge. Over the door beneath the dilapidated curved tile roof hung a horizontal board, covered with swallow and bat droppings, inscribed "The Studio of Literary Contentment". Although Shi Yihai couldn't read it, he knew that the building had originally been the study attached to the mansion.

The person weeping in the study was Jin Qiwen. At that time, she was just coming into the first flowering of womanhood, and although she was plainly dressed in clothes that were far from new, and her face was streaked with tears, her beauty was nevertheless fully the equal of that of any of the lovely women portrayed in the paintings which adorned the mansion.

Young people nowadays probably imagine that no sooner had the 1911 Revolution taken place than the Qing aristocracy simply disappeared in a puff of smoke. In fact, the last emperor's reign dragged on until his abdication was finally promulgated in February 1912, and following this, Puyi (the former emperor) continued to reside in the Forbidden City, living in full imperial style. In 1917 Zhang Xun attempted a restoration, and around that time in the streets of Peking it was quite common to see Qing loyalists swaggering about dressed in full court regalia. Puyi was not expelled from the Forbidden City until 1926 — or the fifteenth year of the Republic, as it was then called — and from thence fled to Tianjin where he set himself up "in exile" as Master of the Zhang Garden. Even then he still regarded himself as emperor, and continued to bestow both peerages and posthumous titles on his loyal followers. Seen in this light, therefore, it was hardly surprising that life in the mansion continued to play itself out, even if only as a centipede continues to wriggle after it is dead.

This, then, was the household into which Jin Qiwen had been born, the daughter of the prince's second concubine. Her mother died of puerperal fever soon after giving birth to her. From her childhood, Jin Qiwen's mind had been filled with restorationist ideas, and the prince and his senior wife never tired of reminding her that she was a princess. Her tutor, as well as teaching her to read the *Biographies of Virtuous Women,* also gave her frequent lessons in the rise, splendour and decline of the Manchu dynasty, in order to inculcate in her the sense of self-respect proper to one

of aristocratic, indeed imperial, lineage, as well as a sense of revenge. Yet the high walls of the prince's mansion could not with-
stand altogether the battering of the tide of the times. Jin Qiwen's
uncle, her mother's brother, was, of all things, a member of the
revolutionary party, and subsequently took office in the government set up by the northern warlords. Two of her three brothers
also became active in society, and turned into men who were the
very antithesis of princes. They took to wearing western suits,
learned foreign languages, and finally ended up by changing their
names and throwing themselves into the kaleidoscopically changing world of affairs.

As Jin Qiwen grew older so too did she increase her understanding of the world beyond the high walls. Now she had requested
permission to attend a western-style school, and had incurred the
charge of unfilial disobedience from the prince. Urged on by her
other elder brother, who saw her as a rival claimant to the inheritance and thus would not be satisfied until she had been disowned,
the prince, in a towering rage, had "sent her to the cold palace"
(the limbo, to which in the old days concubines who had lost
imperial favour were consigned) by locking her up in the study in
the deserted garden, declaring that she would remain there until
she had abandoned the notion of going to school.

Jin Qiwen wept bitterly, and the black-bordered cuffs of her
mauve Manchu-style dress were damp with tears. The fringe which
normally covered her brow was in a mess, and the two loops of hair
which had been caught up on each side of her head had started to
come loose. At one point she had cried herself into a state of
semi-consciousness.

Perhaps it was just as Shi Yihai picked up the sound of her
weeping that Jin Qiwen became aware of the squelching noise
made by his feet as they trampled the yellow clay. She raised her
head and gazed in tears through the torn rice paper pasted over

the swastika-shaped lattice-work window into the garden beyond. Through the gently swaying rushes and clumps of wild rose bushes bathed in the autumn sunlight, she saw that by the wellside, about thirty or forty paces from the studio, there was the figure of a young fellow standing in a peculiar posture, his two rather crooked legs moving up and down as he trampled the yellow clay. A bright girl, she quickly guessed that he must be the servant of the priests from the school next door, and that he was treading the clay to be used for making figurines (she'd heard the steward talking about this). She also saw the torment he was enduring from his punishment, and thinking of the famous line of poetry "Both of us drifters at the world's end, what need have we of a former acquaintance in order to meet now?", she was in an instant filled with sympathy for him; unable to restrain herself, she covered her face and was racked with even more bitter weeping.

At that moment the heavy-featured Qiuyun appeared. She was the last maid to have been born into service in the prince's household. As it moved towards destitution, the household was still determined to extract the utmost from her, and so she had been ordered to look after the two mistresses of the house as well as the princess. She, however, had made up her own mind to devote all her care and attention to the latter, while only going through the motions where the two mistresses were concerned. She stole a lithograph copy of *The Dream of the Red Chamber* for the princess, who, after having read it herself, would secretly tell her stories from the book. They took to comparing themselves with its tragic heroine Lin Daiyu and her faithful maid Nightingale. When night fell and all was still and dark, save for the flickering light of a single lantern, the sound of cold rain beating against the windows and the scampering to and fro of the rats above the papered ceiling, they would press close together, arms around one another as they sighed and wept, pitied and comforted each other. Now Qiuyun had stolen the key to the study and had come to release the princess and to discuss with her what should be done. She suggested that she should run away to her uncle.

Supported by Qiuyun, Jin Qiwen walked out of the dusty study. Just as she was about to turn out of the garden and go back to her own room, she suddenly told Qiuyun to stop. Pointing in the direction of the well, she said:

"People shouldn't be maltreated like that. Go and untie him!" Once she realized what the situation was, Qiuyun went over to Shi Yihai and did as she'd been bidden.

A still autumn afternoon. In the eyes of the universe, of our own earth, so infinitesimal a moment as to have been hardly registered. From the viewpoint of modern history, nothing worthy of record, of analysis or research occurred during that hour on that day. But to Shi Yihai, what happened was an incident of unsurpassed mystery and wonder which he would never forget as long as he lived, and to which he returned frequently in his dreams. He always remembered how Qiuyun was suddenly at his side, and the resoluteness with which she untied the bootlace binding him. Dazed and flustered, he tried to thank her, but Qiuyun simply pointed in front of her and said, "Thank her!" Through the green and gently waving fronds of a weeping-willow tree he saw Jin Qiwen standing in front of a clump of rose bushes, watching him intently, her eyes still damp with tears, her face full of sympathy. As she stood there, a figure dressed in mauve, two butterflies fluttered about her, while a few ginkgo leaves gently floated down onto her shoulders. He stood rooted to the spot, not knowing how to express his gratitude and admiration. But before he had recovered from his trance, Qiuyun had already taken Jin Qiwen by the arm and disappeared from sight.

That afternoon Father Ai'er drank himself into a stupor and didn't wake until noon on the following day. By that time Father

De Taibai had returned, so his colleague did not pursue the matter of how Shi Yihai had managed to release himself. When Shi Yihai returned to his little room, though, his heart was consumed with anxiety. He feared that the princess was shortly to meet even greater misfortune, for he knew full well that what she had done was an extraordinary act of rebellion.

It is now necessary to imagine a much later scene, enacted before the front gate of the prince's residence. The copper studs on the door had withstood the swords of attackers, but had proved unable to resist the kicks dealt by the onward tread of history. The prince, his wife and his concubine had all died, despairing and broken-hearted. Jin Qiwen's elder brother had sold all the remaining property, including the deserted garden, to the church school, and Father Ai'er had also bought the complete set of hardwood furniture from the main building.

On the day of which we now speak, great confusion reigned outside the gate. Three horse-drawn carriages had come to collect furniture and other odds and ends for Jin Qiwen's greedy brother, a fourth had been sent by the now married Jin Qiwen herself to take away her share of the inheritance, while Shi Yihai, sent by Father Ai'er to pick up his furniture, was also there with a large handcart. Jin Qiwen's husband, good-for-nothing but lying at home on the couch smoking opium, or doing the rounds of the brothels in the Eight Big Lanes just outside Qianmen, suspected that the jewellery and other trinkets had not been divided fairly and was refusing to let go of the door of his brother-in-law's carriage. A group of passers-by had formed a circle around them and stared with gaping mouths. The brother-in-law had hidden somewhere else, and his wife, sticking her head out of the carriage window, was hurling curses at Jin Qiwen's husband. After a great tumult, the brother-in-law's three carriages eventually managed to get away, whereupon Jin Qiwen's husband, taking no further interest in the carriage which he himself had hired, headed for the nearest wine-shop.

Jin Qiwen wept quietly in the carriage and gazed tearfully and not without regret at the treetops protruding over the high wall, bidding a silent farewell to the mansion where she had passed her childhood and youth. The wheels of the carriage began to roll, and only then did Qiuyun step onto the running board, carrying a hardwood tea-table. This should by rights have been included in the furniture purchased by Father Ai'er, but Shi Yihai had secretly slipped it off his handcart and given it to her, saying, "Fate hasn't been kind to the princess. Keep this for her." Qiuyun thanked him repeatedly, explaining:

"When the princess still lived here she always used to keep this by the end of her bed. The poor thing, she's never had anyone to care for her, but if she's got this then she'll at least know there are some good people in the world, and that'll help her get through life with a lighter heart…"

The carriage wheels rolled over the hard yellow earth leaving two faint tracks, and as Shi Yihai watched it disappear into the distance, for some unaccountable reason he was overcome by a feeling of emptiness, as if someone had taken something important from him.

At this point we must allow our imagination to transport us once again, this time to a temple fair. A magic lantern show is underway; while the operator alternately sings and shouts in a hoarse and raucous voice, a succession of pictures appear portraying foreign gentlemen dressed in tails strolling with their crinolined ladies beside a distorted vision of Hangzhou's famous West Lake, painted in garish reds and greens. Nearby, the enormous copper kettles and the brass studs on the handles of the mobile sorghum-flour tea stand flash in the sunlight. Beside the stand, beneath a cloth awning patched with a variety of bright colours, a stout old gentleman selling baked wheatcakes stuffed with pork and vegetables is using his pot-scraper to tap out a series of rapid rhythms on the rim of his pan. Making our way past the rings of onlookers gathered about the performing monkey and the patent medicine seller, through the stalls selling odds and ends and old clothes, we come upon the nasturtiums and flowering crab-apples brought by the nursery-men. We enjoy, too, the sight of a cage full of "tiger-skin" parrots carried here by the birdsellers, and a tub of "black dragon eyes" put on display by the goldfish seller. Then, as we approach the principal temple building, under the shade of the bracketed eaves we see a row of vendors with their wares spread out before them: here is to be found every type of antique, porcelain, calligraphy, paintings and inkstones.

How many years have gone by? What is past hardly bears contemplating. Beside one of these displays we see Qiuyun. She has grown quite fat, and her dress bears no resemblance to the Nightingale of former days. She is seated on a small folding stool, stitching the sole of a cloth shoe while keeping an eye on the few pieces of porcelain and jade bracelets spread on the ground in front of her. Now we also see Shi Yihai, already in his mid-thirties; his capacious Chinese-style trousers obscure the arc of his bandy legs, so that his strong and well-proportioned torso gives him a handsome and athletic appearance. He has come out on a shopping errand for the two priests and makes his way towards Qiuyun's "stall". Qiuyun raises her eyes and looks at him, not without a certain wariness.

"What do you want to buy?"

"That blue and white porcelain plate."

"I won't sell it for less than it's worth. You make an offer first."
Shi Yihai puts down a fistful of bills, moist with sweat.

"This is what I've got. Let's say I've bought it, but you keep it for me."

Qiuyun says nothing, but gathers up the money.

"Is the princess getting any better?"

"A bit. She's not coughing so much."

"Heard anything from her husband?"

"No. No point in expecting anything from him anyway." Qiuyun pauses, then adds, "It's just as well he cleared out. Otherwise we'd be in for more disasters."

While Qiuyun and Shi Yihai are carrying on this conversation, a hefty fellow suddenly appears about ten paces away. His arms are bare, his hands are on his hips, and he has a coarse thick red cotton sash wrapped around his waist. His mouth is clamped firmly shut, and he is weighing up Shi Yihai through half-closed eyes, ready at any moment to come striding across with a few broad steps. This man, who at the time of which we speak supports himself by performing with a steel trident and selling snake medicine, will later became a briquette maker at the coal depot and marry Qiuyun.

The stars and constellations revolve in their orbits and the affairs of men run their course. We should now imagine ourselves in the park of the Temple of Heaven at the height of spring. We need not linger by the Hall of Annual Prayer, nor by the Echo Wall, for such are not places for the exchange of intimacies. We escry, instead, a remote corner where the cypress woods are thickest. There is a stone table, surrounded by four stone stools; one of the stools has been broken, so that three people are seated whilst a fourth stands. Jin Qiwen and Shi Yihai sit facing one another. It is already 1958. To reach this point where they are seated at opposite sides of the same table has taken them thirty years. Their joys are insignificant, their sorrows of little account —

but still, their lives and deaths, their songs and tears, should never-theless be allowed to occupy their deserved place in the history of human civilization.

For Jin Qiwen, the long path to this meeting had not been an easy one. Right up until a few months previously, despite her loathing for the husband who had abandoned her and left her penniless, she held to the notion that she was still under an obliga-tion to continue her existence as his wife. She had been greatly shaken by Qiuyun's marriage. In the past she had rather looked down on Master Wang, who was after all a seller of snake medicine turned "coal-blackie", and she had most earnestly entreated Qiuyun to think very carefully before committing herself. Regard-less of how low Nightingale's fortunes fell, she should not have to marry a "Drunken Dime". However, events proved that Master Wang was far from being the Drunken Dime of the novel *The Dream of the Red Chamber*, and living in the same courtyard Jin Qiwen gradually came to envy Qiuyun. To her surprise, the swarthy, hefty and uncouth Master Wang showed himself to be a kind, gentle, honest and simple man, and his broad shoulders and shovel-like hands proved more than able to bear life's burdens and grapple with its problems when things were at their most difficult. When Qiuyun gave birth to a son, Jin Qiwen treated the child as if he were her own, and as she hugged him, kissed him and played with him, her eyes would frequently fill with tears, whereupon she would turn her head away and surreptitiously dry her eyes with her handkerchief. She too needed such human joys!

It was Qiuyun who took the initiative and suggested that she pluck up her courage and find a man to marry. Jin Qiwen was persuaded, and Qiuyun went to court on her behalf, where she very easily completed the proceedings necessary to effect a divorce with the original husband. When Qiuyun mentioned the name of Shi Yihai to her, she lowered her head in thought for a moment —

but why be choosy now? In fact she saw a lot of Shi Yihai in Master
Wang, and the first and foremost feature the two men had in
common was a kind heart. So Qiuyun despatched Wang to tell Shi
Yihai what they had been thinking. Shi immediately concurred,
whereupon it was arranged that they should meet at the spot we
have described.

Although Jin Qiwen had been extremely discreet in her plan-
ning, it had ultimately proved impossible to avoid creating something of a stir in the lane. Qiuyun and Master Wang had set off an
hour earlier than Jin Qiwen lest they arouse the suspicion of their
neighbours. Nevertheless, as she stepped out of the courtyard and
walked up the lane in the direction of the bus stop on the main
street, lightly made up and carrying a bone-framed cloth bag,
people pointed at her and pulled faces, sneered and snickered.
Some even deliberately approached her and asked loudly:

"And whom is the princess calling on today?"

"You're looking very elegant today, Princess, what's the big
occasion?" By the time she reached the street, she was almost ready
to go into the grocery, buy a packet of flavour powder and go
straight home; but imagining the stern look in the eyes of her
indispensable companion Qiuyun, she gritted her teeth and made
her way to the stop where she boarded the bus for the Temple of
Heaven, her heart thumping all the while.

The circumstances of Shi Yihai's departure were entirely different. He had taken the unusual step of expending fifty *fen* on a visit
to the barber's for a haircut and shave, and dressed himself in the
new uniform which he had hardly worn since it was made. The
evening before, he had bought himself a new pair of cloth shoes
specially for the occasion. For three evenings in succession he had
been to the public bathhouse, and he had also cut down on
cigarettes. He hoped that people at the school, seeing how happy
he was, would make enquiries, tease him and even poke fun at

him. But despite his obvious transformation, nobody noticed. That morning as he went out of the school gate to keep his tryst, he had seen Garlic Shoot riding to work on his bicycle, coming straight towards him. From a distance he started to smile, ready to call out a cheery greeting to Teacher Shuai, but Garlic Shoot, although his gaze took him in, seemed not to notice him at all and pedalled rapidly past.

Now, however, Jin Qiwen and Shi Yihai sat facing one another across the table. Although he was already forty-seven and she forty-four or forty-five they were like youngsters in the first flush of love; so overcome, indeed, that they were at a complete loss for words. Seated to one side, Qiuyun looked first at the one, then at the other, and having repeated the motion several times finally issued instructions in an authoritative tone:

"You two just have a good chat. Wang and I are going to take a turn in the park, we'll be back soon. Don't you go your separate ways until we return!"

Master Wang stood behind Qiuyun grinning sheepishly, apparently hoping that a display of his and Qiuyun's happiness would be an inspiration to the seated couple.

Qiuyun and Master Wang set off. Shi Yihai raised his eyes and gazed at the person for whom he had yearned so long. Today the lines on her face appeared far less deeply drawn; her eyebrows were particularly fine, and her eyes were as clear as autumnal pools. The mended jacket she wore, with its pattern of small black flowers over a purple ground, set off her fair neck and face to perfection. Having been instructed by Master Wang to initiate the conversation, Shi Yihai began haltingly:

"It's been many years now, but I've never forgotten your kindness when you saved me that time."

Jin Qiwen glanced at him quickly. His square face could in no wise be described as refined, neither were his brows thick nor his eyes large. Two long lines, traced downwards from each side of his nose, unavoidably emphasized the breadth and toughness of his lips. It was immediately obvious that here was a crude and unlettered man. But equally plain for all to see was his generosity, his vigour, and his reliability. With a wan smile she replied:

"You've done a lot for me since then. Let's not talk about it. I've met too many bad people in my lifetime, and the good ones have been all too few. My heart has been hardened — you could strike a match on it. I don't hold out any hope for a turn in my fortunes…"

Having said this, she panicked. What was she saying, why had these words come bursting forth? She'd forgotten everything Qiuyun had told her to say.

The spring breeze generously wafted the fragrance of the crab-apple blossoms, now in full bloom, into the corner where they sat. Of its own accord, a woodpecker abandoned the ancient cypress which grew beside them and flew off to peck the bark of some other tree. Rainbow coloured gossamer, refracting the rays of the unclouded sun, floated by and was caught in the branches of the cypress. Puffs of willow floss quietly and discreetly rolled by under their feet. What else passed between them not even Qiuyun knew, save for one detail: finally Jin Qiwen handed something to Shi Yihai, an object about a foot long, wrapped in cloth. She told him that it was actually one of a pair, of which she was giving him the one while for the time being she retained the other. Beyond this she did not feel there was any need for further explanation.

Overcome with emotion, Shi Yihai felt as if his heart were about to leap from his chest, and he cursed himself for not having brought a present truly appropriate for the occasion. He had bought two catties of mandarins which he had wrapped in a handkerchief, and these he now passed across to Jin Qiwen. Realizing that once the mandarins had been eaten, nothing would remain, they could not help laughing, he heartily, she with head lowered, using the handkerchief to cover her mouth.

Things having reached this stage, one would have thought that subsequent events would have run their course so smoothly as to provide no further interest. Not so. First Jin Qiwen fell ill, and although she did not die, she seemed to be afflicted with every symptom known to medicine. Such was his desperation that Shi Yihai wished he could ascend to heaven to beg for a miraculous pill from the immortals. It was Master Wang who told him one day that he need not fear for her life; she was going through her menopause, and once this was past all would be well.

So it was that Shi Yihai waited until 1962, when a further disruption occurred. By this time Jin Qiwen was nearly fifty, and the neighbourhood positively resounded with rumours about her. According to the most wounding of these, she had actually undergone a secret abortion two years earlier. In order to preserve her self-respect, therefore, she felt it preferable to remain single rather than to have people mocking her after her re-marriage. She could just imagine the sort of things that would be said.

"See! What did I say? Once a princess, always a princess, they've got to have their pleasures!"

Qiuyun did her utmost to talk her out of this, and Master Wang urged Shi Yihai to get his part of the marriage certificate drawn up.

"If you get yours done, she'll certainly get hers, she won't want to humiliate you."

It was a snowy day, and the large flakes cast a gently undulating veil over the school grounds. Cao, dressed in a heavy padded coat and a furlined hat, was rushing off to the district office to participate in some sort of meeting, when Uncle Shi suddenly appeared before him and called on him to stop. How could Cao have known that it had only been after many days of mental struggle that Shi had finally conceived this plan — to waylay him in the secluded

alley in order to make the request which had assumed such decisive importance for Shi's future life? Uncle Shi had been unwilling
to approach anyone else amongst the school's leadership, but he
felt that old "Darkey" Cao was, relatively speaking, more sympa-
thetic, and would perhaps understand him and help him to arrange things while at the same time respecting his confidence.

"It's cold, Uncle Shi, why aren't you indoors keeping warm?"
asked Cao in amazement, noticing that the snow on the shoulders
of Uncle Shi's jacket was a good inch thick.

"I've got something to say to you," said Uncle Shi, averting his
gaze.

"I've got to go to a meeting," Cao replied. "Don't stand out here
in the cold, you'll catch a chill. When I've got a moment I'll come
around to your room and you tell me all about it at your leisure."

"It's urgent," said Uncle Shi, suddenly fixing his eyes on Cao,
apparently angry.

"Go on then, go on."

Cao inwardly reproached himself for his attitude of a moment
earlier, at the same time wondering what sort of urgent matter
Uncle Shi could possibly have. Uncle Shi, however, did not respond, so Cao went on to ask kindly:

"Is the stove in your room too small? I'll get the general affairs
department to issue you a new one tomorrow, one of those vase
types with the long mid-section. The pupils are always smashing
your window when they play football, aren't they? I'll have the
sports department put some wire netting across it. Is your cough
any better? If the infirmary's out of cough mixture you can go to
the chemist's and buy a few bottles for yourself and I'll make sure
the school doctor reimburses you."

"I don't want any of those things," retorted Uncle Shi, expelling
a gust of breath through his nostrils, "I want ... I want a certificate!"

This time at least Cao did understand, and replied without hesitation:

"Why didn't you say so sooner? I'll write it for you as soon as I get back from the meeting. You really ought to change the padding in your bedcover, but you certainly won't get enough with a single person's cotton ration tickets. I'll give you a certificate so you can get a supplementary allowance."

Cao recalled that Uncle Shi had raised the matter of his need to change the padding in his quilt a fortnight ago.

Looking as if Cao had just given him a blow across the ear, Shi Yihai stamped his foot and silently walked around him and disappeared into the distance. Cao shrugged his shoulders, telling himself that he should excuse the old man his eccentricities, and without further ado set off to his meeting.

Uncle Shi returned to his room at nightfall. He didn't turn on the light, but for a long time sat in the darkness as if in a daze, deep in thought. Even the person closest to him in the whole school could not divine what it was that he needed above all else. In the eyes of others he was probably an outstanding worker, a unionist worthy of commendation, a model for whom "school was home", a classic example of one who worked hard and swallowed injustice without complaint. But beyond all that, no one thought of him as a man, a man who needed a woman. His need was for the commonest and most trivial of human happinesses, a family, however small!

That winter Uncle Shi contracted acute pneumonia and was admitted to hospital. People noticed that he was frequently visited by Master Wang from the coal depot, who brought him thermos flasks filled to the brim with hot chicken soup. During this period, Jin Qiwen's kitchen was frequently filled with the aroma of just this sort of chicken soup, a matter which elicited idle gossip from a certain neighbour sharing the courtyard where she lived....

Just when Uncle Shi had once again plucked up the courage to ask Cao to issue him the certificate he needed for his marriage, the Cultural Revolution broke out, engulfing everything in its path. When he heard that Jin Qiwen's home had been ransacked and she herself made the object of struggle as a "feudal remnant", he was consumed with anxiety for her. He managed to persuade Uncle Ge to let him search through the storeroom where confiscated goods were kept, but he was unable to find the token which matched the one in his keeping. Subsequently, Master Wang told him that Jin Qiwen had buried it in a safe place, so safe that it was as secure as if she had locked it away in her own heart. Hearing this, he was deeply moved. After this, every night when all was quiet and people were abed, Uncle Shi would shoulder a broom and set off to Bamboo Leaf Lane, where he would sweep the area assigned as a punishment to Jin Qiwen, leaving only a little stretch for her to take care of after daybreak.

IX

All this was told to me by Uncle Shi on that unforgettable evening, although naturally his account differed in the style and tone of its telling.

During his narration, I questioned him repeatedly about one thing:

"Just what was it that the princess gave you?"

The flush of wine had not yet completely faded from his cheeks, and in the face of my repeatedly expressed curiosity he was eventually unable to restrain himself from opening his only wooden chest and taking out the foot-long cloth parcel. The veins in his neck pulsated strongly, and his whole face shone with radiant happiness.

"Here it is, here it is."

But when his coarse thick fingers touched the knot, he hesitated. He lowered his head, panting lightly, as if engaged in a fight to the finish in the wrestling arena. He was obviously in great mental turmoil. At last he lifted his head, let out a breath, and said to me sincerely:

"I swore an oath that I wouldn't show it to anyone else... I have to be worthy of the princess."

Without further ado he put the bundle back into the chest, locked it forcefully and then, his forehead covered with large beads of perspiration, looked at me apologetically, a silly smile on his face.

By the time Uncle Shi had finished narrating his long story it was already past midnight. The whole school, the entire city seemed to be peacefully asleep. Only the night wind, blustering about like a drunken man, brought with it from near and far the chirping of insects.

I was stirred by his tale, and no sooner had he finished talking than I suggested that the next day I get Cao and the school authorities to issue the certificate as a matter of urgency, in order to bring the romance to a happy conclusion. Uncle Shi nodded his assent:

"The reason I called you over tonight was because I was hoping you'd lend a hand. The neighbourhood committee has implemented party policy on the princess now, and she's counted as 'one of the people', so I reckon we ought to be able to get this business of ours on the right track at last." Nevertheless, he lay on me a solemn enjoinder:

"I've really poured my heart out to you tonight, so I'm in your hands. You don't have to go running off to Cao tomorrow. When we've worked things out properly I'll give you the word and then you can go and ask for us. But before I give the word you must act as if you know nothing. Don't give me away. Will you do as I say?"

"I'll do as you say," I replied.

"Swear it," he said, fixing me with flashing eyes.

I was more than willing to swear such an oath, and when I had done so he smiled. I had never seen such a happy smile on his face before — he didn't laugh out loud, but his eyes creased up into two crescent moons, the wrinkles formed by the smile were clearly and distinctly etched, and he displayed a mouthful of neat, strong teeth. For the first time, I felt that his face had a distinct beauty. Perhaps there is indeed a law by which happiness has the power to render a person beautiful and kindly.

However, two days later I noticed the old biddy who was chairwoman of the neighbourhood committee come to the school looking for Cao. He only exchanged a few words with her, then sent her off in search of Garlic Shoot. I went over to Cao to ask him what she wanted, and he wrinkled his brow and replied:

"She says they have to host a foreign guest, so she's come to take a leaf out of our book. She was asking about our experience, but how can we parade our 'experience' in public?"

"What foreign visitor's going to inspect the alley?" I asked, my curiosity aroused.

"It's that princess, her husband's come back," Cao replied with indifference. "I hear he's a Canadian citizen now, and he's quite a successful capitalist over there. He's come back this time for the Canton trade fair, and wants to have a look around and do a bit of touring at the same time."

On hearing this I almost exploded, and Cao looked at me in amazement as I quickly tried to conceal my emotion. Throughout the morning I found it impossible to concentrate on my teaching, and once I'd finished lunch I rushed off to Uncle Shi's quarters. Master Wang was just coming out as I arrived — as might have been expected, he had already heard the surprising news.

"How come this Jack-in-the-box has suddenly sprung out of nowhere?" I asked Uncle Shi.

"Perhaps it's me who's the Jack-in-the-box. Let's not talk about this business any more, all right?" he replied severely.

Soon after, a parents' meeting in Bamboo Leaf Lane provided me with the opportunity to gather what relevant information I could. I learned that initially Jin Qiwen had been absolutely opposed to seeing her former husband, since they were formally divorced. However, acting through the street office and the neighbourhood committee, the "relevant authorities" repeatedly urged her to "carry out the revolutionary line in diplomacy", and in the end she reluctantly agreed. In order to welcome the honoured guest, Bamboo Leaf Lane was subjected to a frenzy of cleaning, and the organization responsible for goods confiscated during the Cultural Revolution voluntarily returned everything that had formerly belonged to Jin Qiwen, including the long-legged hardwood tea-table.

The — how should we describe him? For the time being let us call him a businessman — had in his younger days been a dissolute rake, a chronic frequenter of brothels who cared not a whit for Jin Qiwen; so small, indeed, was his regard for her, that in 1948 he had secretly sold the house and property and fled with the proceeds. Yet there is probably nothing under heaven more changeable than man. He escaped first to Hong Kong, and from thence made his way to Canada where, using the money he had brought with him as capital, in one way and another had succeeded in making a fortune. In the struggle for existence he had rid himself of his former vices, and at the same time acquired a certain degree of managerial unscrupulousness. He married a foreign wife, who bore him several children of mixed race, and eventually reached the point where he could crown his successful career with retirement. By this time he was a millionaire, but with the death of his foreign wife and having handed the business over to his eldest son he suddenly felt as if he had wakened after a long dream. Filled with remorse for his excesses, he became a vegetarian and engaged in Buddhist devotions. He ravenously devoured reports of conditions in mainland China and was filled with feelings of homesickness, while the sorrowing face of Jin Qiwen frequently haunted his dreams. Now he had returned, bringing his eldest son with him. He was not being hypocritical; on the contrary, he was motivated by genuine repentance. To all his guides and hosts he sang the praises of the Communist Party and its beneficence, and of the achievements of socialism. Had he been able to do so, he would have laid his heart bare and sworn an oath upon it to devote all his declining powers to the furtherance of the prosperity and wealth of the Motherland.

I was told that this businessman could not hold back his tears when he saw Jin Qiwen alone in her room. He had imagined that she must have spent the past twenty years and more continually longing, night after night without cease, for his return. He solemnly proposed to take her back with him to Canada where she could live out her allotted span, as recompense for his former sins. His guides believed they were about to witness the birth of a beautiful episode in the history of Sino-Canadian relations; and especially when the businessman ordered his Eurasian son to bow to Jin Qiwen, and the long-haired besuited youth obediently bent down before her, they burst out with a spontaneous round of applause.

The attitude of Jin Qiwen, however, was a great disappointment to her former husband.

"It's impossible. I'm used to being alone. Really, I ought to be grateful to you. After you deserted me and ran off with everything, I simply had to learn to live by the sweat of my own brow. In the new society, I came to understand the principle of serving the people. Back in the beginning, I used to strip flakes of mica and glue card-board boxes together, not much of a contribution, I grant you. But now I've learned how to paint eggshells — you can see them on the table here, they're all my work. And look, those certificates on the wall, they were all given to me last year by the Arts and Crafts Corporation. The decorated eggs with coloured landscapes are sent to Canada amongst other places and earn foreign exchange for the state, not to mention boosting our country's reputation. I feel comfortable in myself leading this sort of life. Now you've come back to China to see me and to apologize for the wrong you did me. All right, I won't hate you for it anymore. I hope from now on you'll be able to do a lot of good work."

The Canadian businessman did not lose heart, however, and before leaving he said: "Think it over again. Neither of us are getting any younger, and even though you are serving the people, you really ought to retire. I'm ready to come back to get you at any time."

As a consequence, the neighbourhood quickly started to hum with all sorts of rumours about the princess's imminent departure for Canada.

One day in late summer, when the evening sun was setting, I went to seek out Uncle Shi in his room. He never locked the door, and no one who went to call on him ever needed to knock. Pushing the door open and entering as I always did, I found the room quite empty. Uncle Shi was nowhere to be found. I wandered somewhat disconsolately out of his room, and leaving the school grounds, began to stroll through the quieter and more out of the way lanes. Clouds resembling red and gold cotton balls filled the sky, and the intoxicating scent of silk-tree flowers was carried on the evening breeze. Turning into a lane flanked by several tall Chinese scholar-trees, I saw a young girl, her hair braided into two plaits, stooping low as she swept up the seed-pods which had fallen in profusion on the ground around the trees. Just as I was wondering why so many seed-pods had fallen someone suddenly emerged from behind the thick trunk of one of the trees bearing a long bamboo pole with a grappling hook attached to one end. I called out a greeting as I walked towards him.

Seeing it was me, Uncle Shi put down his pole, and wiped the sweat from his forehead with his shirt-tail. Pointing to the girl, he said, "This is Ge's daughter."

Turning to her and pointing in my direction, he explained:

"One of the teachers from the school — say hello."

The girl was tall and thin, with features that made me recall Uncle Ge when he was still alive. She greeted me, and I asked, "Have you been reassigned to work in the city?" She blushed, and replied in an embarrassed tone:

"No. Things are difficult for Mum on her own, so Uncle Shi's fixed up this pole for me and taught me how to get the pods down from the trees. We sell them to the medicine shop — the extra money helps a bit."

Actually, in the past I'd often seen people gathering seed-pods from the scholar-trees, but I'd never stopped to think why they were doing it. I suppose I had a vague notion that they were from the Bureau of Parks and Gardens. Only now did I realize that in this city of ours there were still ordinary citizens like this, who in order to supplement their meagre material needs, gathered seed-pods, caught ground beetles, collected waste paper and melon seeds....

I joined Uncle Shi in helping her for a while, and after seeing her load a full basket onto a little wheeled cart and trundle it off into the distance, I finally headed back to the school with Uncle Shi and entered his room.

Raising the matter of the princess, I advised him simply to go ahead, apply for his certificate and get married. Uncle Shi sat there calmly. He had reverted to his old pipe-smoking habit of years ago, and as he quietly puffed away he said to me with great sincerity:

"Old Wang brought a message to say that the princess is of the same mind. But just now I can't. I've got to let things cool down a bit and give the princess a chance to think this business through properly." We sat together in silence. Neither of us had anything more to say.

At first I didn't look at him directly, but instead fixed my gaze straight ahead, where I found my eyes focussing on a large bamboo broom behind the door. The handle was already worn down to a shiny burnt yellow colour, and the straw had turned an ashen grey. For the first time in my life I discovered that a broom could give rise to a host of rich associations and deep emotions. I thought how the broom daily sacrificed itself to make the world clean and beautiful, tirelessly sweeping away what it disliked while leaving behind untouched what pleased it; and yet when the ground and paths refreshed the eye with their cleanliness, the broom must needs be hidden away in a corner out of sight.

I felt a wave of gentle emotion welling up within me, and as it gradually strengthened into a surge of passionate feeling I turned my gaze upon Uncle Shi. His profile resembled a stone statue, richly imbued with love and strength.

Here there were no violins playing beautiful melodies, no guitar or mandolin accompaniment, nobody reciting symbolist poetry, no Michelangelo frescos or sculptures by Rodin; neither were there roses in full bloom, nor budding jasmine; no babbling brook was audible, nor the sound of wind in the pines; absent too were any clouds of sandalwood incense, neither were the pure tones of the ancient lute to be heard: only an uncultured, physically unprepossessing bachelor in his sixties — a soul of the utmost simplicity, crystalline in the purity of his honesty and generosity. Yet it was he who caused my heart to swell with poetic emotion, music to sound in my ears, the scent of fresh dew to fill my nostrils. He was the distillation of the beauty of pure humanity.

X

I telephoned Cao from the publishing house to tell him that the text of the funeral oration was ready, and that I would be at the school before long. I also told him, "There are a few people from outside the school who should be invited to the memorial meeting."

The note of surprise in his voice could be heard through the receiver:

"From outside the school? Who? Uncle Shi didn't have any friends or relations."

"Yes, he did," I replied. "I'll tell you when I get there." Cao seemed partly to understand, and said to me, "You probably knew how he came by what was wrapped up in the bundle that he left. Get over here quickly and solve the riddle for us — the whole school's been talking about it for the last two days."

I went there by trolley-bus. No sooner had I got off than by sheer coincidence I ran into Garlic Shoot and a few other teachers, and together we made our way through Bamboo Leaf Lane to the school. Garlic Shoot was holding forth in a loud voice on the subject of the mysterious object left behind by Uncle Shi, and delivered himself of an absurd supposition:

"Haven't you seen a *ruyi*? You know, it's that sort of a what-d'ya-call-it you often see laid out on top of the low *kang*-tables in the Palace Museum, about two feet long, the thing looks like the sign for 'similar to' in geometry, the big end's shaped like a *lingzhi* fungus. I went round to Cao's yesterday to have a look at Shi's — it's made of hardwood and inlaid with precious stones — emerald, beryl and the like. How could he have got hold of a thing like that? He probably picked it up during the Cultural Revolution when the pupils left the things they'd confiscated lying around all over the place. A bloke like Shi would never actually steal anything, but when he came across a valuable thing like that staring him in the face he was still smart enough to wrap it up and hide it away safely! So you can see that in a commodity society even the most honest people find it hard to resist the lure of wealth!"

At this point he wrinkled up his eyes and laughed loudly.

At first I hadn't paid any attention to Garlic Shoot's peroration — I was too absorbed in self-reproach over Uncle Shi's death. After I'd been assigned away from the school, despite the distance and the busy workload I really shouldn't have allowed so much time to elapse without going to see him. Even on those few occasions when I did visit him, why did I always confine the brief conversation to generalities instead of settling down to spend the whole night in intimate conversation with him?

However, when I realized what Garlic Shoot was saying, I felt as if someone had plunged a dagger into my heart and, unable to control myself I yelled at him:

"What the bloody hell are you talking about?"

Garlic Shoot responded in typical fashion, with a shrug of the shoulders and a smile. He said nothing, but raised his eyebrows, presenting a picture of innocence. The other teachers asked no further questions, and for a while we all walked on in silence, the only sound that of our footsteps.

Suddenly I heard a burst of sobbing, which gradually swelled into loud weeping. It was coming from the door of number 14. The sound of crying whirled heavenwards on the autumn wind, seemingly embodied by the dead leaves caught up together with it.

The weeping voice beat against my heart, against my throat, against my eyes. It all came to me. A person dies, another weeps heartfelt tears for him. What could be more commonplace in this world? And yet, from the sound of these tears, from the unfulfilled love of those two people which belied the auspicious promise of the *ruyi* cherished by each of them, I could nevertheless grasp something — something that makes possible the continuation of the entire human race, something that enables this world of ours to be more beautiful, more pure.

The princess's weeping was anguished and unrestrained, evoking in me the most powerful response. I struggled with all my might to contain myself, but in the end I could not, and with a howl I burst into tears like a child. Garlic Shoot and the other teachers were dumbfounded. They stared at me with incomprehension as if I had been stricken with some affliction of the mind.

I walked on, crying bitterly.

If only people could understand when they hear me crying.

Surely they must.

January-February 1980
Weeping Willows, Peking

Zooming in on 19 May 1985

Near midnight on 19 May 1985, Anthony Barker, the Peking correspondent for Reuters, rushed to his telex machine without even pausing to wipe the sweat from his brow. He sent out the news of the day: a riot had occurred in the Chinese capital after a China-Hong Kong soccer match.

It was the most hair-raising experience Barker had ever had. A crowd of soccer fans furious at China's unexpected defeat had surrounded his car: "One fan shouted: 'Which is better, China or Hong Kong? Answer wrong and I'll kill you.'"... He also reported that "the crowds of mainly young men yelled: 'Get the foreigners, get the foreigners.'"

As with any incident of this nature, the first report of it in the international media is sure to be regarded as the most authoritative. On the following day the Hong Kong press gave the story front-page coverage, and some papers highlighted Barker's contention that this was an example of Chinese "xenophobia". The *Oriental Daily* described the scene as follows:

> Thousands of soccer fans surged through the streets outside Peking's Workers' Stadium chanting anti-foreign slogans, stopping foreigners' cars and accosting foreigners.

The Kuomintang's Central News Agency sent out a wire story which delighted in quoting local Hong Kong soccer fans to the effect that:

> They are shocked by the xenophobic tenor of last night's events in Peiping... They have woken up to the fact that the Communist Party of China could not cope psychologically with defeat at the hands of the Hong Kong team, and that this led to this anti-foreign outburst... As a result, Hong Kong people are more anxious than ever about the future of the territory.

In fact, this was by no means the first instance of disruptive behaviour authored by soccer zealots in Peking in recent years. On 18 October, 1981, following Kuwait's three-nil victory over China, Chinese fans waylaid and jostled foreigners' cars; on 12 November that same year, after a Chinese victory over Saudi Arabia, soccer fans thronged into Tiananmen Square, scrambled onto buses they'd ambushed and started screaming and dancing on their roofs. Some also jumped from the bus roofs onto sedans, crushing the tops of two cars. On 1 July 1983, after defeat at the hands of the Mannheim soccer team, local supporters threw various objects at the victorious team, and stopped foreigners' cars outside the stadium.

Not only did the 19 May Incident of 1985 lead to a shocked response both in Hong Kong and internationally, on the following day it was the subject of high-level concern in China itself.

A New China News Agency report dated 20 May cited the misbehaviour of some "rotten apples" who threw things onto the playing field and caused disturbances, wilfully destroying public property outside the stadium. It went on to say that:

> What is even worse is that a small number of people waylaid foreigners' vehicles near the stadium and showered them with insults.

It also announced that the leaders of relevant government bodies had said:

> Last night's incident is the worst of its kind in the history
> of sport in the People's Republic, and the most damaging
> to China's international image. This type of ignorant and
> brutish behaviour is quite out of keeping with the stature
> of our capital city. The legal organs of the Peking Munici-
> pal Government will be energetic in their application of
> the law to all offenders.

One can only imagine that Anthony Barker woke up the next morning feeling very pleased with himself. We should recognize the legitimacy of his intentions: a desire to maintain an objective and fair stance in reporting the incident. But in his article he got at least one thing wrong: he claimed that the fans threw tomatoes onto the field. According to the detailed statistics compiled by the relevant authorities, the following objects were hurled into the stadium from the stands (with a capacity of 80,000): 2,995 plastic drink containers, 156 glass bottles, 143 loaves of bread, 13 broken bricks, and 15 apples. Tomatoes were selling for over two *yuan* a kilo that day, and they were in short supply.

Public Security officials detained and questioned suspects the moment the stadium opened its gates. Over 30 people were detained during the game, and more than 90 were arrested during the rioting outside. On 20 May the New China News Agency gave the official number of arrests as 127.

Originally, Hua Zhiming wasn't particularly interested in the match that night.

On the afternoon of the 18th he had been in a great mood. He finished his daily production quota in the morning, and after hanging around the workshop for a while in the afternoon he told his foreman he was "splitting " early. The foreman tried to give him a hard time, but he knew Hua was a bit hot tempered and once stirred could start an explosive argument or even pick a fight. So in the end he let him go without a word. Hua sped out of the factory on his bike like greased lightning, heading for the public bath house. They had one in the factory too but he didn't want to let on to any busybodies that he'd got off early. After a really good wash he changed into the clean clothes he had with him in his canvas gym bag, and leaving the baths he set out for Zhengyi Road, just over from Wangfujing, the street that had been planted with trees earlier than any other part of Peking. The green strip down the centre of the street with its trees, shrubs and lawn, divided by a path, created a restful scene.

Hua had arranged to meet his girlfriend there at six that evening. It was still early: five past five.

He was twenty-six, yet in all those years he'd never taken a stroll by himself. Of course he could walk, but he had no idea what it was like to go for a walk alone. He could have taken the opportunity that now presented itself to stroll down the path pushing his bike; alternately, he was free to lock his bike and go for a walk by himself. But this was beyond his ken. He carelessly parked his bike and found himself a bench to sit on, and whipped out a packet of cigarettes which he proceeded to smoke his way through.

Three sculptures had been put up on the green strip that ran through Zhengyi Road during the runup to the 1984 National Day celebrations. One of them — a woman street-sweeper made out of imitation bronze entitled "Cleaning the Street" — had been toppled by someone in early May and broken into three pieces. Another one, "Tuning the *zheng*", of a woman playing the Chinese horizontal harp, had a middle finger broken off, and someone had coloured her cheeks with red ink and painted a necklace around her neck. "Study", the third sculpture, was of a girl reading. Her lips had been painted bright red. Hua was sitting near the comical figure of this girl, but as he never took much notice of the things around him he had no idea what had happened to the statue... The only girl he was thinking of was Xiao Yingzi.

They'd met at the movies three months ago. He put on a show of being a real live wire; it's a method he'd used to make lots of friends, though he knew full well that someone like him, whether it was on the free market of love or going through a matchmaker, was not much of a success with girls.

Only one week before the 19 May Incident, in the "Marriage Marketplace" column of the 13 May edition of *Peking Science News* you could find the following sort of advertisement:

> Unmarried woman of 26, 1.61 metres tall, university grad-uate, technician in a local research institute. Good features, healthy and pleasant disposition, looking for a mate under 30 who is locally employed, has a college or higher degree, is outgoing and trustworthy, 1.7 metres or taller.

What hope could someone like Hua Zhiming who was only 1.65 metres tall, have when a woman shorter than him wanted a man over 1.7? People often jokingly referred to him as being "physically handicapped". But he'd had the courage to make it with Xiao Yingzi. She was 1.61, and had "good features, healthy and pleasant disposition". Also, she had no qualms about his height, and wasn't picky about his academic record either...

Believe it or not, Hua just sat there puffing away for over half an hour. Of course his brain hadn't stopped working, but at the same time you couldn't say he'd given himself up to fantasizing either. Xiao Yingzi was ten minutes early. They couldn't appreciate the little games lovers play: you know, purposely arriving ten minutes late for a date, or dropping some comment calculated to make the other person feel jealous, and so on. They were real friends. Of course, by now they knew it was not as simple as that: they knew they were "a thing".

Xiao Yingzi had taken more care than usual over her appearance today, though it was wasted on Hua Zhiming. She noticed his khaki Safari jacket, his light blue shirt and the gold and red striped tie which she'd never seen him in before. She coquettishly sidled up to him, and Hua caught the faint smell of milk about her. She cleaned bottles in a dairy. No matter what camouflaging perfumes she used on her hair or skin, there was always a whiff of milk about her. Hua Zhiming actually liked the smell; but he never told her. He was capable of expressing only the most superficial thoughts. This proved he was an average bloke, but deep inside him weren't there also some beautiful misty poems?[1]

They walked down the street pushing their bikes and went for dinner at the Pine and Bamboo Restaurant on the southern corner of East Qianmen Avenue. As usual Hua Zhiming wanted to order enough dishes to cover the table, but Xiao Yingzi kept him in check. It was her way of showing that she was already thinking of "his money" as "our money"; Hua could only conceive of it as being proof that she was "a true buddy". As they were about to set off to his place, Hua Zhiming told her: "I want to give you a real good time. I'll take you to see a video show."

On returning from work that day, Hua's father noticed something was amiss the moment he set foot in the door. He shouted out to his wife, who was in the kitchen preparing dinner, "Where'd that gizmo next to the telly come from?"

Hua's mum came rushing out of the kitchen with a bottle of cooking oil in her hand. She knew her husband could explode at the drop of a hat, and she spurted out, "Zhiming brought it back at lunchtime, said he borrowed it from his classmate Xiao Mengzi.

---

[1] "Misty poetry" is the favoured form of modernist writing among China's romantic avant-garde.

Didn't his father work in Japan for a while? Brought this back with him. It's a machine for showing videos. Now I told Zhiming not to borrow such things, we couldn't pay for it if it broke. But he..."

"The nerve! That son of yours is out of hand. But go on, go right ahead, keep on spoiling him..." He interrupted her with this furious outburst.

The oil in the wok was beginning to splutter, so Hua's mother had to disengage herself from the argument and rush back to the kitchen. The father plopped himself down in their newly acquired "Italian" settee, and lit up a cigarette with a quivering hand. French, Belgian and Italian style imitation leather sofas were all the rage, and he took no exception to this type of innovation in his environment. There was even one in the dairy products store. Video recorders were not so common, and he fixed his gaze on the shiny new piece of equipment with disgust. He was like a shepherd confronted by some ungainly new creature in his paddock.

There are different levels of conscious activity: the superficial level deals with sensory perceptions and consciousness, leading the mind to react to exterior stimuli with simplistic — often merely positive and negative — reactions or judgments. The next level of ratiocination is concerned with analysing the pros and cons of issues. And just a little deeper down is where the layer of thought informed by past experience and the "collective unconscious" merge. Hua Zhiming's brain only functioned on these levels. He was not deep; he's what you'd call a "superficial thinker". But his father was another story: given his relationship with his peer group he could relate to society at large; he was capable of near-rational thought based on the analysis of particular data; he also engaged in philosophical musings inspired by disjointed and random thoughts. These levels of thought were not independent and isolated but intermingled in complex, ever-changing and three-dimensional patterns. As he sat glaring at the video machine, the

father's mind was ticking over: the very strangeness of the machine
— both its physical appearance and the nature of its function —
brought to mind recent legal cases involving pornographic video
screenings. Then there was Xiao Mengzi's dad. He was one of
those technician types who had been allowed to join the Party, was
promoted and then sent overseas. He'd used the chance to get a
few things for himself. To Hua's father, a cadre who had never
exploited the perks of office, there was little difference between
Mengzi's intellectual father and the self-satisfied and cocky illegal
profiteers out on the streets. Then his head filled with images of
what he saw as the confusion and spiritual pollution created by the
Open Door and Economic Revitalization policies. As a loyal Party
man he felt a sense of spiritual fulfilment in actively supporting the
policies of Party Central, but again he found it agony to square this
with the disturbing developments he saw taking place in his own
family. Complex and contradictory emotions and thoughts min-
gled, clashed and exploded in his brain, sending his blood pressure soaring and putting him so much on edge that just about
anything could have set him off. So when Hua Zhiming strode
breezily into the room in the company of a woman who was just as
alien to the father as the video machine, the old man went right off
the handle.

I'll leave the details of the ensuing scene to your imagination.
Hua's mother was an indispensable lubricant in the machinery of
conciliation, and despite the emotional scene Xiao Yingzi stayed
for a while out of respect for "auntie". But she was deeply hurt. She
couldn't understand why Hua Zhiming hadn't told his parents
beforehand: it was her first visit. She couldn't remember what
Hua's father had been railing about, though it shocked her very
much: it seemed that at home Hua just didn't count. The mother
finally herded her son and his girlfriend into Hua's small bedroom
shutting the door anxiously while she tried her best to calm the old

man: she told him that dinner would be ready soon and coaxed him off to their room for a short rest. She made him some tea, heated some water so he could wash his feet, and did all she could to humour him. Finally she slipped in a few words on her son's behalf: "We should be happy that the boy's finally got himself a girl, and she seems a decent sort... considering his education, job, looks and personality, well, it's a good thing he found someone... What are you doing by blowing your top the second she walks in the door?..."

Meanwhile Hua was sitting across from Xiao Yingzi in the cramped room smoking silently. Xiao Yingzi was leafing through a shoddy pirated edition of a martial arts novel, *Wonder Woman from Snowy River*. Hua was hopeless at expressing his feelings, although he was not even aware that the situation demanded some sort of explanation. Xiao Yingzi left after a while. Only long after the lingering scent of milk had vanished entirely did it occur to Hua Zhiming that they hadn't fixed a time and place for their next date.

An uneasy silence finally settled on the household. In the normal course of events, the mother would watch television; tonight she knew better. Some time after nine, Hua Zhiming slinked out of his room, his hair a mess. He'd decided to cheer himself up with a video. It was the first time he'd operated one of those things by himself, and he couldn't remember what button to press first. No matter how much he fiddled around there was no trace on the blizzard-stricken screen of the Hong Kong martial arts movie Xiao Mengzi had lent him. "Fuck this. What a rip off!" He was angry with Xiao Mengzi and he gave up trying.

The next day, Sunday 19 May, was one he would never forget. He went over to Xiao Mengzi's place first thing to return the video set and the cassette. Naturally, he started out by ticking his friend off, but Xiao Mengzi lost his head when he discovered that

Zhiming had managed to erase the whole cassette, one that was on loan from someone else. Hua Zhiming was dumbfounded. He couldn't remember what buttons he'd pressed, so he was in no position to defend himself. Just his luck; everything was going against him. He didn't take it out on Xiao Mengzi though. "How much will it cost me to make it up to you?" he asked. Xiao Mengzi told him 150 *yuan*. Hua went straight home without another word, took 180 *yuan* out of his room and went back. He handed over the 150 without a shudder. With the other 30 in his pocket he rode his bike around aimlessly.

An observer would probably conclude that Hua was looking for a way to vent his frustration, even though he hadn't the self-awareness to realize this himself. He didn't want to go home, that's all. Sure, he knew where Xiao Yingzi lived, but he'd never set foot in the place (although she'd promised to take him there the following Saturday evening), and he certainly wasn't about to force his way in now. He just wanted to get this Sunday over and done with so he could give her a call at work the next day. He didn't want to go to the park; as we've observed he was oblivious to the attractions of nature. There were a few exhibitions on at the China Art Gallery; he passed by it without noticing what they were. He vaguely felt like dancing (but it was only a stray impulse, as a shorty he knew full well that you had to be tall and long-legged to look good dancing). But where could you dance? Ordering a tableful of food at a restaurant, a few pints of beer, and leaving it all half eaten was Hua's normal mode of self-indulgence. But since he'd known Xiao Yingzi that all seemed dumb. So all that was left was the movies. He'd seen the American 3D movie "Gunner Hart" twice already, as for the latest local product "Code Name 213" he wasn't sure it was worth the thirty *fen* to buy a ticket. Better to find a place with video games, but the only spot he could think of was in Zhongshan Park and here he was all the way off in Dongdan. The last thing he wanted to do was ride back. This was the big capital. And nowhere for Hua Zhiming to go to let off steam! As he rode on out to Jianguomen, where all the foreigners live, passed the International Club, the Friendship Store, then the Jianguo Hotel and the Hotel Beijing-Toronto, something occurred to him: Chinese like him weren't allowed into any of those places. Then he thought about Foreign Exchange Certificates, and about how he and Xiao Yingzi had been looking at the hard currency counter in the basement of the Xidan Bazaar the other day. They'd bumped into one of those jokers who works the black market in foreign currency at the bottom of the stairs.[2] He had a pointy chin, but was tall, over 1.7m. The second he laid eyes on them they could tell he was giving them the nod to do a deal. Hua ignored him and led Xiao Yingzi in past the guy. Hua had seen what was for sale, he had the desire but not the wherewithal to buy... Then he thought of the Great Wall Hotel which he'd seen on TV, and what Xiao Mengzi had said, "In Guangzhou you can get into any place you want as long as you have dough." He thought of that advertisement he'd seen by chance in the Guangzhou *Yangcheng Evening News*: "The China Hotel presents a concert by Zhang Delan...[3] with the backup of break dancers, best songs, best dancing, tickets available for only ¥25 and ¥30." He remembered at the time someone explained what the ¥ meant, but he still couldn't work it out.

These ruminations were, however, coterminous with his trip to the end of that part of town. Around Dabeiyao there were so many individual entrepreneurs' stalls on the footpath that the languorous pedestrians were forced to walk in the bicycle lane. Somehow

---

[2] Most dealers in the foreign currency black market in Peking are from Xinjiang and are part of an underground network.

[3] A Hong Kong singer.

or other Hua's front wheel hit a man in his late forties. The fellow swung around with a mean look on his face and spat out:

"Clean up your act, slob."

Honestly, he didn't light into the guy. Sure, Hua got off his bike without a word of apology, but wasn't his silence enough? Then someone else's bike struck his back wheel and he turned around without even looking clearly and shouted:

"Are you blind?"

The fellow he shouted at was about his age and they started arguing loudly, each exchange getting nastier, although nothing too much out of control. Hua didn't recall whether anyone tried to stop them; nor does he recall what they said to each other. All he knew was that by the time he turned into the Third Ring Road he couldn't have been in a fouler mood.

The 21 May edition of the British *Daily Mirror* had a commentary on the 19 May Incident entitled "Throwing Stones", and in a speculative tone concluded:

> Are there not among these Chinese soccer fans some dis-
> affected ex-Red Guards who committed acts of violence
> during the Cultural Revolution period?

This is typical of the responses from abroad.

We should point out, however, that the Cultural Revolution broke out in 1966 and the first three years were the most violent. The majority of Red Guards were in senior middle school or university at the time, that is from seventeen to twenty-three years of age. By 1985 they were thirty-six to forty-one. Yet, the eldest of the 127 19 May Incident detainees was thirty-five; while there was a small number of people in their thirties, the majority were young people from fifteen to twenty-five. At the start of the Cultural Revolution they were infants or hadn't even been born. No, they were not "disaffected ex-Red Guards".

There was also no lack of speculation about the rioters within China, first and foremost in Peking itself, not among other soccer fans but among middle-aged and elderly people, including many cadres. "Is it all linked to price increases?" they queried. As everyone knows, starting on 10 May some consumer items were subject to "upward price adjustment". Naturally, this had quite an impact on consumers, although it hurt older people most. Of the people detained during the incident few were married, most were unattached or even entirely ignorant of the process of courtship. Most of them were still living with their families and had never had to do any shopping for things like meat, fish or vegetables. Although their wages and bonuses were low, they had a reasonable disposable income because they were living and eating at home for free. Their spending patterns were also different from their elders: they judged goods on the basis of taste and whim rather than merely on price. All in all, it's hard to provide convincing evidence that the incident was a protest against state economic policy.

It wasn't entirely accidental that Hua Zhiming ended up at the stadium that night. In the first place, he enjoyed spectator sports. One reason he wasn't as caught up in the regional competition for the Eleventh World Cup as he would have been in the past was Xiao Yingzi. She didn't like sports. The second was that he thought there was no real competition.

After a meal at the Phoenix Restaurant on Guanghua Road, he rushed over to the Workers' Stadium and bought himself a sixty *fen* ticket from a scalper for two *yuan*. By this stage he was in a pretty good mood again. As long as it's a draw, he thought to himself, China wins this heat. Anyway, Hong Kong had never beaten the Chinese national team, and tonight China would have everything going for it. They were sure to give the Hong Kong barrackers something to moan about.

Hua squeezed his way into the stands, found himself a place and looked around at the crowd. People were holding up home-made banners with legends like: "China Must Win! On to Mexico!", "Fans from Tianjin Support the Team", "Score a few goals for us, Gu Boy" (the meaning of this escaped Hua for a moment until he realized they were talking about Gu Guangming). Suddenly the stadium exploded: some people in stand number two held up a banner reading "China: 2 - Hong Kong: 0". Hua felt elated, and he waited anxiously for the Chinese team to appear. Every goal they scored would help him get rid of that build-up of frustration in his chest.

There was a white-haired man sitting to Hua's right, a true soccer fan. The proof of real devotion was whether you went to the training ground next to Langtan Lake to watch your favourite players at practice. This old boy would go whenever he had the time. There are about two or three hundred "super fans" like him. They often gathered outside the wire fence at the training ground long before the players appeared. And once a training session was over and the players left, the fans still hung around wistfully, reluctant to leave, discussing the object of their passion among themselves. They are like the parents of students who are about to take the university entrance exams, ever ready to serve their children food or give them a pick-me-up. They derive some personal fulfilment from watching the students study for exams. Need I even say that all of these "super fans" were there on the night of 19 May?

The old fellow on Hua's right had come well-prepared: transistor radio, high-resolution binoculars, push-button umbrella and the latest edition of the tabloid *Soccer*. Once the match began he sat there listening to his radio and talking to himself while he watched the game. On Hua's left was someone who looked like a high school student. He acted as if he were sitting on a pin: every few minutes he jumped up from his seat, and even when seated he swayed from side to side endlessly. Every once in a while he would pick up a colourful toy horn and blow it with all his might in support of the local team. But none of this annoyed Hua Zhiming because the old man let him use his binoculars. The lad sitting in front of Hua was holding two pigeons wrapped in a handkerchief; he was just waiting for the Chinese team to win so he could release them.

Hua Zhiming didn't do anything unseemly during the game. He was like a drop of water that followed the ebb and flow of the crowd's emotions. The mood changed suddenly because everyone was completely unprepared for what was happening on the field: the Chinese team was losing. The psychological shock had an extraordinary effect on the crowd's collective unconsciousness: there was ceaseless hooting and shouting, and then without any prompting tens of thousands of people started stomping their feet in unison, the sound echoed through the stadium. Eighteen minutes into the game when the Hong Kong team scored a goal there was a momentary silence, as though the entire place had entered the eye of a typhoon; but when the Chinese team won a goal in the thirty-second minute of the game, the wild tide of rejoicing reached a peak. UPI summed it all up the next day in their report saying that "every time the Hong Kong side got control of the ball there were violent calls from the spectators and wild shouts". But it wasn't only the fans who were carrying on like this, or even the other players and coaches who were sitting on the sidelines. Even the police who were there to maintain order were obviously caught up in the wild barracking for the local team. Defeat was unthinkable and they wouldn't even countenance a draw — they wanted victory, nothing less than a decisive victory. So even when the Hong Kong team gained momentary control over the ball there was mass outrage, as if it were an unconscionable insult. This attitude can, in part, be attributed to the excessive emphasis on national dignity in Chinese reports of sports competitions. If there is a victory or a record is broken it is spoken of as "China Taking Off"; defeat or mediocre results are construed as nothing less than a "National Shame". Zhu Jianhua bore this sort of psychological burden when he competed in the high jump at the 1984 Olympics; and the tens of millions of Chinese viewers watching him approach the bar on TV saw the jump as symbolizing either China's national revival or its defeat. But he didn't make the grade. In the 19 May Incident there was the same type of mass psychological pressure — a pressure exerted by the eighty thousand fans present — that increasingly undermined the Chinese team's game. When the Hong Kong side scored another goal in the sixtieth minute of the second half, fans who had all been anticipating a frenzied celebration at the end of the match lost control altogether. The atmosphere in the stadium became hysterical. The heavens added to the maelstrom by sending along a sudden downpour. Some spectators without umbrellas moved under the cover of the stands, but the majority stood out in the wet in furious defiance, some even stripped off and danced around wildly in the rain screaming until they were hoarse. In the last quarter the national team fell about itself and lost two to one. At the end of the match, the spectators stood up as one, a sullen wall of fury. The face of the old boy next to Hua was awash with tears; the student on the left had trampled his horn underfoot long before this; the lad in front ripped off the tails of the pigeons and let them go. They had flown away dripping blood, some of the feathers landing on Hua's face as they went. That's when he noticed plastic drink containers flying overhead onto the playing field.

The intoxication of victory allowed the Hong Kong team to ignore what was going on around them. Although the Chinese team didn't want to shake hands with them (some foreign reports emphasized this point), in fact the Hong Kong players hadn't given a thought to such niceties themselves. Sweaty and tearful they hugged each other and shouted for joy, and they were joined by supporters, other members of their contingent and reporters wildly celebrating their victory. They had endless pictures taken of the team in different configurations, but to the spectators the flashes of the cameras were like gloating eyes piercing the dark. All of this hit hard at the pride of the locals. You can imagine the emotion as that sullen wall of fury banked up and began to topple.

The emotional tide spilled in a number of differing directions. A small group of dyed-in-the-wool fans moved straight for the exit where the local team would be leaving the stadium. It was a mournful party, and one hears it was led by a few white-haired old men. They sobbed at the police who wanted to hold them back begging that Zeng Xuelin, coach to the national team, "show himself and answer some questions". Although this group was spearheaded by some of the older, more rational fans, those who pushed up behind them out of curiosity were quite different. They responded with direct disobedience when they saw the police trying to get the older fans to leave quietly. This mindless mob thought they were in the right and believed the people upfront were heroes willing to confront the situation. They started to grunt. The national team had been pelted with plastic drink containers when they had left the field, and someone, thinking a member of the team had come out to talk to them decided to throw some more garbage. There's no telling who took the lead, but within seconds the whole ignorant mob was screaming out foul and angry curses: "Fuck the National Team! Fuck Zeng Xuelin!"

Meanwhile another group was taking it out on the Hong Kong side. Only when the Hong Kong players attempted to leave the field did they discover that they had been surrounded and it was only with the help of guards that they were able to find a route out of the place by going through the VIP box. Curiously, they all had umbrellas and they used these as shields to break out of the encirclement — it took two attempts — and withdraw to the changing rooms. The stadium workers had thought the VIP box would be the safest exit because the terraces behind it (numbers 17, 18, 19) were reserved for organized groups and not for the average fan. Ironically, this was the spot where the only real "bloodletting" of the evening occurred. Someone hurled a glass bottle from terrace 17 and the Hong Kong player Cheung Ka-ping held up his arm to protect his face. His mouth and fingers were cut by broken glass.

Yet another group directed their displeasure at the police on duty. The latter had originally been primed to deal with victory celebrations; the last thing they were ready for was a crowd enraged by defeat. Anger made the job of controlling the mob even harder and the efforts of the police only provoked increased fury, shouting and, as the mass surged out of the stadium, irrationality: somebody broke a window near one of the exits.

The whole incident was both simple and complex. On the one hand it was an explosion of mass hysteria born of the competitive spirit, something that is above nationality, race, politics and morality. The complex side of it includes psychological elements peculiar to the Chinese people involved: thirty years of political and economic instability have cast a shadow over everyone; because of the Cultural Revolution China has a generation of young people who are culturally and educationally deprived in the extreme; Chinese society lacks avenues for people to let off pent-up frustrations; there is the energy of individual liberation released by the present Open Door policy, and the repressive opposition to this, something that has been little studied ... and so on.

Hua Zhiming had gone along with the mob, caterwauling all the way out of the stadium. The cool evening air had brought him to his senses somewhat. He heard the sound of breaking glass; the police were running towards it. But the strangest thing was what he heard next: from somewhere around the north gate of the stadium came the sound of an emotional voice singing "The Internationale" and "We Workers are Powerful"!

Those songs and the extraordinary energy of their singers somehow set Hua Zhiming off; everything came rushing out at once: the video tape, the 150 yuan he'd forfeited, Xiao Mengzi's pettiness, his father's glare, Xiao Yingzi's discomfort. Then there were the white tear-drop earrings she had been wearing last night. This reminded him of milk, and its soft fragrance. He felt he'd really been done over. Then he thought of the cock-up the Chinese team had made tonight. All Li Huajun and Zhao Dayu could do was pass the ball and break through the Hong Kong defence; even "Gu Boy" had seemed weak-kneed. And the Hong Kong team was so up itself; they'd have Foreign Exchange Certificates for sure. Then Hua recalled that black marketeer at the Xidan Market; that Jianguo and Beijing-Toronto wouldn't let him in; that you could see the ritzy chandeliers and restaurant through the window, and the waitresses in their revealing cheong-sam dresses. He tried to imagine himself and Xiao Yingzi sitting there, but then wiped the vision from his mind. Without realizing it he was already outside the metal fence around the stadium, and he hardly noticed he'd crossed the street and was approaching the intersection at North Sanlitun...

Was the 19 May Incident really an expression of xenophobia? Was the encirclement of the Hong Kong team a sign of what lay ahead for the territory after 1997? The *Hong Kong Economic Journal*

said it was a renewed expression of the spirit of the Boxer Rebels.[4]
Was that reasonable?

"Local products", however, were the object of most of the vio-
lence: the dozens of large rubbish bins along the road outside the
stadium were all tipped over (they could all be used again once set
right); the glass in a police box was broken; the buses waiting
outside to take away spectators had their windows broken; and
apart from all of the broken glass at the stadium, the "epicentre",
damage extended to a radius of at least one kilometre, reaching
the underground station at Dongsi Shitiao on the Second Ring
Road, where the glass in the doors was smashed as well. Some
policemen were kicked and punched as they arrested troublemakers, although no one had to be hospitalized. And apart from the
Hong Kong player Cheung Ka-ping's cut, no foreigner or Hong
Kong-Macao compatriot was hurt. Even Cheung's injury required
no more than an application of iodine.

It is said that at least one elderly foreigner fainted in his car in
response to the melee outside. Of course, we should all apologize
to him. However, starting the next day countless Chinese, in particular young people, began to feel an indescribable and oppressive
psychological pressure because of the incident. Some units supposedly called for everyone in their employ who had been there that
night to register their names; others say that even if you hadn't
gone to that game you still had to take part in the educational

---

[4] The Boxer Rebellion of 1900 was a violent, anti-foreign popular movement that led to a siege of the legation quarter in Peking. The Communist
Party approves of the patriotic nature of the uprising and views it as a
precursor of their own peasant revolution. The Boxers, rebels who believed
they were possessed of supernatural powers which enabled them to defeat
foreigners, are a symbol to many of indigenous Chinese xenophobia and
mindless mass hysteria.

campaign that was begun as a result. People had to sit on wooden benches at meetings where they were expected to express their indignation at the "rabble rousers" and ringleaders, ending with personal pledges to obey the law. There were also rumours that in future soccer tickets would not be on sale to the public: work units would buy block tickets and thus be held responsible for their own people, selecting only "civilized individuals" for the privilege of watching games. There were also the usual exaggerated tales about the draconian punishment to be meted out to the offenders: all 127 were supposedly going to have their Peking residency permits revoked and be sent into exile in Qinghai.... Fortunately, later developments indicated that the relevant authorities are gradually learning to do things by the book, dealing with the incident in a restrained fashion. Thus, the wild speculations concerning internal exile and the like proved, in the end, to be nothing more than rumours.

Again it was Anthony Barker, the man who had sparked the speculation on xenophobia with his first report, who, having calmed down somewhat, reported on 20 May that "a British diplomat discounted any particular anti-Hong Kong sentiment.

"Whoever it had been, the Chinese would have been disappointed at not going through to the next round of the World Cup."

During their interrogations the Chinese authorities naturally concentrated on the matter of jostling foreigners and stopping their vehicles. Yet virtually none of the people in custody said they had been involved, and hardly any had been detained for this. Most were arrested for throwing 20-*fen* plastic drink containers in the stadium. Some had done nothing more than throw paper aeroplanes into the field or in their excitement refuse to leave the stadium.

On 21 May, the Hong Kong press began to publish more balanced accounts on the incident. The *Ming Pao* said: "Soccer fans throughout the world create disturbances... such incidents have very little to do with the society at large. There's always a group of people in any large city who are ill-educated, emotionally unstable and who are not particularly rational." The *Overseas Chinese Daily* commented: "Soccer riots are the result of emotional excess; they have nothing to do with the state of civilization or public manners of a place. To say that this incident had harmed the image of the people of Peking would be a gross exaggeration."

It is impossible to ascertain from the reports which of the people detained was the one Anthony Barker described in his first report as being a xenophobe. The most serious offence among those arrested was the throwing of bricks at a truck carrying a police back-up team; another was the overturning of a taxi, the only car that was flipped over during the incident.

Hua Zhiming had actually left the stadium and the whorl of fury that had overwhelmed it. Originally, the fates had no desire to see him go under as a result of this incident, however, he realized he'd forgotten his bike. He also found he was walking in the wrong direction. This only served to make him feel worse. Just at this moment a group of rowdies appeared at the T intersection up ahead. Their fury perfectly matched Hua's own frustrated anger. He ran over and joined them without so much as a second thought.

There were about thirty people in the group, most of them Hua's age. They wanted to see some action, or at least create some. They stopped every passing taxi, shouting and jeering all the time. Following repeated questioning from the investigating officer Hua was, with difficulty, able to recall that there was a tall, skinny fellow who had been particularly vociferous, shouting: "Fuck it, while I spend my hard-earned money to go to some lousy game, these guys are sitting in their cars pulling in a coupla hundred bucks a night. Get the sonsofbitches!" From this we may conclude that the "collective unconscious" of the mob was fired rather by jealousy of those who have been making a lot of money than concerted anti-foreign sentiment.

The mob waylaid a taxi and the driver jumped out with his hands clasped in supplication. "Come on fellas, let me go. I've got a quota, can't afford to stop ...."

They let him go on his way.

Another taxi was stopped. This time the driver stuck his head out of the window to plead with them:

"Hey guys, can't you just leave me out of this. I've got a passenger here, you know, and if anything happens I'll be in the shit...."

They beat the car doors, others kicked the boot, some spat on the vehicle. Hua Zhiming just stood by hooting. After a while they let this car go as well.

From what he could remember, Hua said it didn't seem like they were picking on cars with foreigners or Hong Kong people. They were not, after all, the same as the Boxers who had appeared in Peking eighty-five years earlier. Now *they* were xenophobes. Remember their oath:

Heavenly spirits, earthly wraiths
We plead all masters to answer our call:
First, Tripitaka and Pigsy,
Second, Sandy and Monkey,
Third, Erlang show your might,
Fourth, Ma Chao and Huang Hansheng,
Fifth, Mad Monk Ji our ancestor,
Sixth, Liu Shuqing the knight-errant,
Seventh, Flying Dart Huang Santai,
Eight, Leng Yubing of the past dynasty,

Ninth, the Doctor Hua Tuo to cure all ills,
Tenth, Pagoda Bearer Devarāja, and the Third Prince Naṭa
to lead 100,000 heavenly troops...

This chant is proof that in their own unlettered fashion the
Boxers wanted to evoke the force of every symbol in traditional
Chinese culture. Hua Zhiming and these rioters however had no
leadership, plan of action, organization, or aim. They were simply
a mob excited by football fever. If they were to have a chant, it
would probably go like this:

Heavenly spirits, earthly wraiths
We all want to have a good time
Let's evoke Xi Xiulan, Zhang Mingmin,
Wang Mingquan, Xu Xiaoming;[5]
Let's watch (the TV series) "Huo Yuanjia"
and "Love Ties Together the Rivers and Mountains".[6]
We want jeans,
We want disco and Huazi Cosmetics,
We want Sharp, Toshiba and Hitachi electrical appliances,
We want Suzuki, Yamaha, plus Seiko and Citizen...

They are the most ardent consumers of popular Hong Kong
culture and Japanese consumer goods. The real reason they target-
ed foreigners and Hong Kong people during the incident was that
they dislike the way these people enjoy special privileges in Peking
and flaunt their superiority. What the mob was expressing was a
long-repressed resentment and jealousy.

...Another taxi appeared. It was a beige Citroen. Again they

---

[5] The names of Hong Kong pop singers.
[6] Hong Kong television soap operas.

surrounded it and forced it to stop. The driver jumped out and told them off in no uncertain terms:

"What do you think you're up to? What's all this fuss about?"

"Get the sonofabitch!" someone shouted. They went for the driver and he took flight...

Hua Zhiming was still hooting mindlessly, though he was feeling much better now.

"Let's turn this motherfuckin' car on its head," someone cried. Hua Zhiming applied himself to the task enthusiastically, taking up a position by the rear wheel. Hands that should have been embracing Xiao Yingzi clasped the rear mudguard. Then with someone shouting out directions they began to turn the car over. Their first attempt failed, the second time around they had it on its side.

A policeman came running over and the mob dispersed. Hua put no particular effort into making a getaway; in fact, he walked over to the other side of the road at a calm, lackadaisical pace. He felt as though all that built-up tension had disappeared. His conscience certainly wasn't bothering him: he'd never been in trouble with the police before so he wasn't scared of them now. This was the best he'd felt all day...

By the time the policeman had appeared most of the mob had disappeared into the crowd of bystanders, although one large fellow grabbed hold of Hua Zhiming's wrist and shouted at the approaching policeman. "Here's one of them, no doubt about it!"

Hua Zhiming was shocked to his senses. But he went quietly. The fellow who had grabbed hold of him had been looking on as the mob had done its work. He hadn't been at the game, he was a government cadre who had been passing by on his bike. He'd waited until the police were in range before taking action in case Hua tried to slip away, although Hua hadn't given escape a thought. His outraged captor overestimated Hua's desire and ability to resist as he took off his leather belt and bound the young man's hands behind his back. Hua was taken to a temporary enclosure. The police didn't have time to take note of all of the details of the stream of detainees. As the morning approached, however, they were divided up and shipped off to detention centres. Only then did they discover that Hua still had his hands bound. Hua had made no attempt resist, nor had he denied his involvement in the incident involving the car.

Two days later he was officially notified that he'd been arrested. Due to the clear-cut case against him he was charged under articles 157 and 160 of the "Civil Code of the People's Republic of China".

There's a tendency in China to lay more store by international reaction than local opinion. The Hong Kong press doesn't require translation, and in the case of foreign correspondents in Peking their reports have the added authority of being eye-witness accounts. The information they disseminate is regarded with the utmost seriousness by the Chinese government. Even foreign (and here I include the Overseas Chinese, and Hong Kong and Macao compatriots) rumours carry with them inordinate authority. Foreigners told us about Chen Jingrun, a mathematican who had achieved startling results in his work on "Goldbach's Conjecture". Accordingly, Chen became a national hero. Yet as far back as 1961 a middle school teacher by the name of Liu Jiaxi solved the famous "Kummer Problem". In 1980, this same teacher's work on "Steiner's Tree" was of the highest international level, but because no foreigners told us about it we let him die in poverty in October of that year.

Anthony Barker's report on the 19 May Incident probably had a lot to do with the authorities declaring it to be "the most serious, nationally humiliating incident" since the founding of the People's Republic of China. In fact, apart from the cases mentioned earlier, in 1981 when the Chinese women's volleyball team beat both Japan and the USA in the Third World Cup, a mob of young people had demonstrated on bikes in Tiananmen Square; others had gone to the Japanese and US Embassies in Peking to shout anti-foreign slogans. At the time reports were made to the state leaders but because there was no strong international reaction, added to the fact that China had, after all, won the world title, no effort was made to investigate.

We need to be more rational in our responses; more notice should be taken of local reactions, in particular those of our own people, especially young people, regardless of whether they are direct or indirect, pleasing or offensive. If a country is constantly annoyed by its youth, is concerned solely with lecturing them and never bothers to listen to them, then that country is suffering from senility...

As soon as they returned to Hong Kong, Kwok Ka-ming, the Hong Kong team coach, spoke to the press. He said, "What happened on 19 May is no big deal. This type of thing happens all the time overseas. The fans were disappointed at China being knocked out of the competition." The Reuters Wire Service for which Anthony Barker worked dropped the story thereafter as their attention was taken up with the Brussels soccer disaster of 29 May. There was a clash between supporters of the Italian team Juventus and the British team from Liverpool, in which thirty-eight people lost their lives (thirty-three Italians, four Belgians, and one Frenchman), over a hundred were hospitalized, twenty in serious condition; and after the match some British supporters threw a table through a shop window and stole goods to the value of ten million Belgian francs or US$160,000. Another British supporter was hospitalized with knife wounds to the stomach; and when the police took action to quell the rioters a Juventus supporter actually fired a gun at them.... Mrs Thatcher called the chairman and general secretary of the British Soccer Association back to Britain and demanded that they not send any teams to Europe for at least two years. The British government made reparations to the families of victims to the value of £250,000. The trouble-makers were, of course, dealt with according to the law; and there is nothing to indicate that any of those involved, whether British, Italian or Belgian, gave a moment's thought to what China's reaction to the disaster might be. Moreover, nobody, from Prime Minister to prole, seemed to think that this incident was a blot on their "national image"...

On 29 May, the Chinese national team was temporarily disbanded.

On 30 May, Yuan Weimin, head of the State Sport Commission, and the famous athletes Lang Ping and Li Ning spoke to ninety of those detained during the incident, emphasizing "the need to enhance our nation's moral traditions, and to resist emulating those bad things from overseas". On the same day, a brick wall was built around the area where the national team trained, replacing the original wire fence.

On 31 May, the Chinese Soccer Association accepted the resignation of Zeng Xuelin, coach of the national team.

From 1 to 4 June, most of the young people who had been detained were released.

Xiao Yingzi had been waiting for a call from Hua Zhiming since 20 May. On 25 May, a Saturday, she couldn't stand it any longer: she rang up his factory. The person who took the call was extremely off-putting: "What is your relationship with him? Come on, you playing dumb or don't you really know? Huazi was nabbed by the cops...'cause of the 19 May Incident. National shame, don't you know. Yeah, he's really in the shit this time. We're all pleased as punch. 'Bout time he got his."

Xiao Yingzi felt positively faint. She was ringing from a public booth, and she leaned against the glass wall and closed her eyes just long enough for her heartbeat to slow down a little. Then she rang her office and asked for the day off saying she had an appointment to see a doctor. It was the first time she'd ever lied to them. Then, still in a daze, she went for a long, aimless walk. Somehow or other she ended up at the green strip where Hua Zhiming usually waited for her. She sat on a stone seat. A group of Young Pioneers were cleaning up the statue of that reading girl; Xiao Yingzi started crying, the tears rolled down her face. She took off her white tear-drop earrings and held them in her hand tightly....

She didn't know where they were holding Hua Zhiming, nor did she have the courage to try and find out. She still hadn't told her family that she had a boyfriend; and she was too embarrassed to go to his place to see what had happened to him. Nor did she know about lawyers. In fact, she didn't have any close friends to confide in. Like Hua Zhiming she was a member of the generation that had been despoiled by the Cultural Revolution. She started primary school during all the chaos, and because of the "education revolution" she received only a scant education in middle school. Her class had to wait for employment, after which they got assigned jobs as workers. They had grown into adolescence in a state of minimal mental activity. Are they really the uneducated generation which gives us such heartache? But apart from criticism, discipline, and punishment, shouldn't we also ask ourselves whether we owe them something? For example, more understanding, concern, and love?

Xiao Yingzi couldn't get a medical certificate to make her absence legitimate so she lost her May bonus. In June for the first time in her life she started reading the newspapers in search of information about the 19 May Incident. She took to reading the papers on the billboards in Wangfujing Street, after which she'd go to Zhengyi Road to sit in the shade. She still hadn't plucked up her courage to visit Hua in jail; nor did she dare turn up at his home. In fact, she still didn't dare tell her parents or any of her friends about it. One thing she had decided on was that she'd wait quietly. She often bit her lower lip now, and had an expression on her face that betrayed both deep worry and determination.

Let's just consider this for a moment: how would the Chinese people be judged, both by ourselves and the rest of the world, if on the night of 19 May at the end of that game the Chinese spectators had accepted the score with equanimity and applauded the out-standing efforts of both sides, then left the stadium quickly in an orderly manner, returning home contentedly?

6 June 1985
Weeping Willows, Peking

White Teeth

I tried an experiment to see if I could stop talking for an entire month.

Everything went well the first day. I didn't say a word at work, neither at the entrance to the building, nor in the corridors, the office, or the dining room, even though people did say a few things to me. All I had to do was to nod, shake my head, smile, or frown to take care of them. When I got home, my mother started in with her usual babbling, so I lowered my head and buried my face in my rice bowl, and paid no attention to her. As for my father and younger brother, they rarely spoke to me anyway. After dinner, I took a shower and brushed my teeth, and then went to bed and read for a while before falling asleep. Though I had a few dreams, I didn't say a word in any of them.

The next day I ran into a few difficulties. These were difficulties I had brought upon myself; they had nothing to do with external factors. That afternoon in the office, I started getting a bit fidgety. At first I thought that my colleagues might wonder why I hadn't spoken a word for two days. But as it turned out, it was me who started wondering why they didn't notice my silence.

By 5.30 nearly everyone in the various offices of our work unit had gone home. Lao Zhan, Miss Peng and I were the only ones left.

It suddenly occurred to me that I shouldn't be carrying out my experiment so passively. Better to take the initiative and get people to talk to me first, and then respond with silence. This test would determine if my experiment was a success.

I brought a pile of report forms over to Lao Zhan.

Lao Zhan is our vice-department head. He's been a vice-department head for eight years now. During those years, we've had three different department heads, but he still has a "vice" stuck in front of his title. There's little chance he'll ever be promoted to department head, and I doubt he even dreams about it. His head reminds me of one of those wide-mouthed red ceramic vases with twin handles you sometimes see in antique shops.

When Lao Zhan noticed me standing before him, he appeared surprised. In the past, he frequently had to remind me to hand in my report forms, but on this occasion.... I thought he might say something to me, but he quickly turned away and sat there stacking the pile of report forms I had given him by tapping them on the glass surface of his desk. Lao Zhan's desk was always a model of organization. In his own leisurely way, he stacked up everything that was stackable, and then arranged the stacks on his desk in a highly orderly fashion. I hadn't finished filling in those report forms. Lao Zhan was already stacking them in a neat pile and arranging them properly on his desk, and didn't check them. He said: "Uh... We'll hand them in tomorrow morning," but he didn't even glance at me, which suggested that he had nothing else to say, so I moved away.

I made a detour to Miss Peng's desk, pulled over a chair and sat down. Miss Peng was getting ready to leave. She had lost one of her knitting needles and was trying to find it. She had to mobilize every muscle in her body to do this, and jerked about like a wind-up toy robot with an overwound spring. When she located the needle under a chair, she sighed with relief. Then she noticed me, and said quite seriously: "It's impossible to buy good knitting needles like this around here." This statement required no response. If I really wanted to test myself, I would have to find another way. So I spread out a newspaper in front of her, and tapped my finger audibly on a front-page article about the organizational streamlining taking place in a certain province.

Miss Peng recoiled from the newspaper as if a caterpillar were crawling on it. A few days ago, in this very office, when I had said out loud: "This entire organization needs streamlining!" Miss Peng had flinched in the very same manner. And then, after wiping the disgusted look off her face, she argued the point briefly with me, developing her logic as follows: "Who's going to streamline who? If you kick a few people out you still have to pay them their salaries, right? If you pay them, why not let them come to work? And if they show up for work, why not give them a little something to do? And if you do that, why not let them do what they've always done? And since this is what happens anyway, what's the use of streamlining in the first place? I've seen it a thousand times. First they streamline people, then they give them their jobs back. Once the first bunch get their jobs back, they hire more people. Once they hire more people, they streamline again, then they give the same people their jobs back, and hire more people...." At this point in the argument she stared at me, as if to suggest that I had gotten my job during one of those fire, re-hire, and hire-more-people cycles. Actually this was the case with me.

Having refused to look at the newspaper article, Miss Peng had sighed and smiled at me, and then got ready to go. I could tell from her expression that she was relieved that I had merely pointed out the article and refrained from discussing it with her.

I went back home with my lips sealed. My mother gave me one

of her customary distressed looks, which can be expressed as "hope plus disappointment divided by two".

Coming home at the usual hour meant that I didn't have a boyfriend yet. I can't stand being classified as an "aging young woman". Who was the genius who thought up that title?

That night maintaining my vow of silence was easy because I didn't really feel like saying anything.

Five days elapsed before someone said to me: "You don't seem as lively as usual." It was as if he had just discovered America.

This was our department head, a man in his prime, a bureaucrat among bureaucrats! The rumour was out that he was about to be promoted to vice-bureau chief. His promotion, however, would have been due neither to his ability, which was of the most common ilk, nor to any particular aptitude for flattery and bootlicking, but rather on account of his extraordinary mediocrity. So mediocre was he, in fact, that when the two opposing factions in the bureau were attacking each other at one point, both sides went out of their way to claim that he had done no wrong, and even praised him for his integrity. During the process of nominating and recommending people for the post of vice-bureau chief, both factions naturally attempted to eliminate possible candidates from the opposition; but because it was impossible to prevent the opposition from doing the same thing, both sides ended up nominating the head of my humble section, the very man standing before me now, for the coveted post.

I was deeply moved by his comment, which made me see him in an entirely new light. For five days, not a soul had mentioned my silence. And here he was expressing concern for me. Maybe he wasn't such a mediocrity after all.

I had always felt that his looks were so mediocre that it was impossible to identify any distinguishing characteristics, but now I discovered a tiny mole next to his nose. This infused his face with new life, and gave him a radically new appearance.

I almost broke my silence and said something to him about it. We were standing in the corridor. A few colleagues who happened to walk by us seemed surprised to discover me standing there face to face with the section chief.

Had the section chief asked me to accompany him into his office, I probably would have had to call off my experiment. But he did no such thing, even though the spot where we were standing was a good bit closer to his office than to mine.

While I was hesitating he began to speak to me: "....those fish-balls they make in your home town are ab-so-lute-ly delicious. When I was there I ate 'em every day, couldn't get enough of 'em. They say the best dish down there is Buddha Jumps Over the Wall.[1] Sorry I never got a chance to try it...."

The section chief had returned from a business trip to Xiamen a week ago. All traces of the fish-balls he had eaten there had long been evacuated from his digestive tract, but when he saw me that was all he could think of to say.

Perhaps if he went on, he'd have something else to say?

No, it seems, that was all. He took out a neatly-folded sky-blue handkerchief and wiped his nose and mouth with it, whereupon I discovered he actually had no mole next to his nose. What I had spotted earlier was probably a toasted sesame seed left over from breakfast. Once again his face was entirely devoid of any memorable features.

When he went back into his office, I lingered in the corridor,

---

[1] A stew, popular in Fujian province, containing pork, mutton, chicken, duck and seafood so named because its odour supposedly enticed the Buddha away from his meditation, and he jumped over the monastery wall in order to taste it, thus breaking his vegetarian vows.

not knowing what to do.

Why wasn't I more lively? Did he sincerely want me to be lively? Ten days before he had left for Xiamen, I had handed him my proposal for reform, a piece of work I had put all my heart and soul into. Hadn't he read it? Perhaps the great tragedy was that he actually had read it, and had made up his mind not to respond to it. He knew that I had made many photocopies of my proposal and had distributed them among the bureau leadership. Now I knew he had handed in his copy to the leadership without expressing an opinion on it.

He was patient enough to wait for someone to serve him Buddha Jumps Over the Wall; he would never jump over the wall himself.

Better to avoid speaking to people like him entirely.

As I walked back into the office, I heard the second half of a sentence that the speaker was quite urgently bringing to an end: "...it isn't worth her while to oppose us."

The voice belonged to a contemporary of mine, a member of the opposite sex. In present-day Chinese society, his chances of survival and advancement were a heck of a lot better than mine. But of late he had been treating me as if I were some kind of a thief. This must have been because when I announced my proposal for reform in front of the entire office staff the other day, I had said something straight off the shoulder to him: "Actually, our two jobs could quite easily be done by one person!"

For some strange reason he reminds me of one of those new-fangled revolving electric standing fans that works as a humidifier and gives off a pleasant scent as well: on hot days he cools you off and relaxes you; on chilly days he can make your flesh creep. Last year when the former bureau chief was in hospital, he had gone to see him with an expensive bouquet of American carnations he had bought with his own money. At that time, there was a rumour circulating to the effect that the ailing 58-year-old chief was about to be promoted to vice-minister. Then earlier this year, this now-ex-bureau chief, who had turned fifty-nine and handed in his application to retire (which naturally killed his chances of being promoted to vice-minister) fell ill again. At the time I had asked my contemporary if he wanted to visit him in the hospital with me, and he turned to me with a big smile and said: "Oh, damn it! I really should go, but there're a few things I've got to take care of. When you see him, give him my best."

When I walked into the office, all conversation ceased. I wanted to tell my contemporary that when I had said that our two jobs could easily be done by one person, I didn't mean that he should be kicked out and I should stay on. Actually I had been thinking about quitting my job for a long time. China's a big place, full of opportunities, especially in the south. The reason I didn't quit was because the moment I left, they'd put someone else in my place. "Our" job, which didn't need two people to do, was just right for two people whose specialty was twiddling their thumbs all day.

My contemporary gave me a questioning look from beneath his droopy eyelids. Lao Zhan was once again neatly stacking a pile of report forms with elaborate precision. Miss Peng stopped revising a memo that was on her desk, and for no discernible reason picked up the tangerine stuck in her teacup and turned it around once. I suddenly realized that the original inspiration for the department head's remark, "You don't seem as lively…" came from my contemporary, who had very shrewdly dropped a hint or two. I felt sorry for him. If I were him, I'd simply get the hell out, or else put my shoulder to the wheel and do something constructive for the bureau. In either case, he would have accomplished something real. Was his job here — his rice bowl — so very precious to him?

My experiment with silence now entered its sixth day. While I was in the bureau cafeteria eating lunch, Sangsang suddenly showed up and sat down next to me.

Ever since I've known Sangsang she's always done her hair like Cleopatra, in royal Egyptian style. This particular hairdo evoked a different response from every level in the hierarchy of the bureau. Sangsang and I worked in different departments. We spent most of our time together in the cafeteria.

When she sat down I got the feeling that my experiment with silence was about to confront its greatest challenge. When the two of us talked, we were constantly interrupting each other, and our conversations often got so loud that people nearby would turn their heads and stare. Of all the people in the bureau, I enjoyed talking with Sangsang the most. The main difference between us was that she had known many people involved in the arts, while I couldn't name a single artist or writer among my friends, class-mates, relatives or neighbours.

Sangsang's conversation topic today was "Depression in the Art World" — actually her own personal depression, since her latest boyfriend happened to be a rising star on the literary scene. To quote a sample of her thinking: "It's almost impossible for Chinese literature to attain international status. Painting, music and film communicate with universal symbols. But Chinese literature's made up of a bunch of odd ideographs strung together and only a handful of foreigners can understand them. As for translations, Chinese and Western society and thought patterns are so different to begin with that it's nearly impossible to bridge the gap. Take stock phrases like 'during the land reform', or 'the year the Anti-Rightist Movement began', the sort of thing that shows up all the time in Chinese fiction. Translating things like that can drive you batty, you need endless footnotes. And once you start with foot-notes in fiction, no one is going to want to read it. You heard the one about the foreigner who saw the line 'During the Great Leap Forward' and asked, 'What's this about the big jump ahead?'"

I listened to her, nibbling at my lunch and smiling at her once in a while. I had great sympathy for Sangsang, and especially for her boyfriend. They wanted to establish contact with the world outside of China, and yearned for things like Eternity and Immortality. They were entirely correct in their views, thoroughly laudable. But the obstacles in their path were immense.

I wondered why Sangsang wasn't surprised by my silence. She didn't seem to notice anything different about me. While she kept up her non-stop monologue, the food in her bowl grew cold.

"...I told him he ought to write about the working conditions here, the grey office building, the grey days, the grey expressions on people's faces, everything so lifeless, grim and dull.... I said he should make it symbolic and abstract and allegorical, so people all over the world could understand it. Bureaucracies are the same everywhere. You've heard of Parkinson's Law? But he doesn't want to write about fashionable topics. He thinks people are tired of reading stuff like that. Lately he's been writing about the colour of the sky, you know, the nearly transparent brilliance of the deep-blue sky...."

I came very close to interrupting her, since I recalled reading in some literary magazine that a Japanese writer had won a prize for a story called "The Nearly Transparent Brilliance of the Deep-blue Sky".

"...I've had it up to here with this place. My boyfriend says he's going to try to find me a better job. But you know, considering the fact that we live in a bureaucratic society, we're doing pretty well here. We're up there on the full bureau level. Foreigners don't give a damn about stuff like that, they can't understand our system anyway, but for us it's everything. You know how it works: county supervisors and regiment commanders in the army have the same status as department heads in a municipal bureau or chief secretaries in a bureau office; heads of prefectures and division commanders in the army get the same perks as bureau chiefs in a municipal government or department heads in a central government ministry; and provincial governors are up there on the same rung with ministers in the central ministries... Every rank has its own perks. A department head gets three bedrooms and one sitting room; a bureau chief gets four bedrooms and one sitting room; a vice-minister gets five bedrooms and a sitting room; and a minister gets a whole traditional house and courtyard for himself. Department heads can travel in a hard berth on a train and charge the ticket to the office; bureau chiefs can travel in a soft berth on the train and charge plane tickets to the office... As for hotel accommodation, department heads get an eight-*yuan* allowance, bureau chiefs fifteen *yuan*, right? And that's not all. When those guys get sick and go to the hospital, department heads have to stay in a room with eight beds, vice-bureau chiefs get a four-bedded room, bureau chiefs get a two-bedded room, vice-ministers get private rooms, and ministers can have a whole suite of rooms to themselves. Then there's all that rigmarole about the kind of car you get driven around in, whether you get a phone at home, how much *renminbi* you can exchange for foreign currency when you go abroad... My god, my boyfriend's been saying that if we started our own business, work our butts off and could save up about 15,000 *yuan*, we could buy ourselves an apartment with three bedrooms and a sitting room. But in the end it's a hell of a lot easier to hustle a bit in a bureau like ours, hook up with the right people, and wangle a job as a vice-department head and be assigned the same sized apartment that way. Hey, you don't have to pay any maintenance fees. What a drag! It's enough to drive you crazy! But that's the way the cookie crumbles..."

She was in such a state of depression by now that she finally noticed I hadn't said a word. Interrupting her "Ode to Inertia" she raised her eyebrows and said: "You're not feeling well today?"

I smiled and shook my head, so she pressed me no further. She took a bite of her lunch, muttered "It's cold," picked up her bowl and left.

Now it was my turn to be depressed. I realized that even though our conversations in the past had seemed rather lively, she was only interested in letting off steam, and didn't really care about what I had to say. Now I regretted having been so open with her.

It wasn't till I left the office that I realized it was Saturday. All the bus stops were mobbed with people, so I decided to walk home. In this way I'd arrive a little later than usual, and my parents would think that I'd been out on a date with a man. This would have fulfilled their sense of self respect, or should I say, vanity; it really had nothing to do with me.

The pavement was so packed with pedestrians that it was often necessary to walk sideways just to get by. I was terrified that someone would stop me and ask for directions, in which case I would have to reply. What a silly way to spoil my experiment! Fortunately no one asked me the way. Nor did anyone even look at me. Something occurred to me in the midst of that great tumult of people: all social intercourse is involuntary. Human beings are basically solitary creatures. If you ask me who suffers the least among the blind, the deaf or the dumb, I'd say the dumb.

Just before I got home I remembered I needed to buy some soap. In the past, whenever I bought soap or other daily necessities I didn't have to speak to the shop assistants. I would simply point to the soap I wanted, hand over the money, and wait for the shop assistant to give me the soap and the change.

I walked into the department store. There were no customers at the soap and toothpaste counter. I leaned on the counter and waited patiently for the shop assistant to come over and help me. There were two of them behind the counter, standing about two metres away from me, chatting up a storm. I waited. They glanced at me, but continued chatting away like hens. I thought to myself: It's their job to serve me. But at the same time they were probably thinking: It's her job to ask for help. Since both parties refused to fulfill their respective obligations, better to drop the whole matter. As I turned to leave, one of them muttered through her teeth, "Sick in the head!"

Normally something like that would have made me angry, but today I was in a particularly balmy mood. Maybe my experiment with silence was a form of mental illness.

I made a long detour and finally got home. My parents were watching television in the front room. When I walked in my mother came up to me and asked: "You had your dinner, didn't you?"

Her eyes were brimming with hope.

I was starving, but I nodded.

My mother was visibly relieved. Trying to appear casual, she asked me: "You ate by yourself?"

I shook my head. She exchanged glances with my father, who was sitting on the sofa.

Heading for my room, I passed by my younger brother's room and noticed him sitting at his desk with his back to the door. He had his hands over his ears, and was memorizing something from a book. The lamp on the desk cast his distorted silhouette on the wall; it looked like a giant spider. He was in his final year of high school, and was preparing for the university entrance exam. The fact that the government could no longer guarantee college students jobs after graduation had hardly dampened my brother's determination to go to college, and had even less effect on my parents. My brother told me: "Even now every university student pulls strings and goes through the back door to get a decent job. People even come to Father for help. Who needs the government anyway? If they offered you a job teaching middle school, would you take it? You got to be out of your mind!" Then he added, oblivious to the fact he was insulting me: "It's pathetic the way you spent two years getting that equivalency degree from Television University. I want a real degree." That reminded me of all those formulas Sangsang had recited at lunch-time. Actually, she left out a few things: 1 technical high school degree + x years on the job = section head = university lecturer = 2 bedrooms + 1 sitting room; 1 technical college degree + x years on the job = department head = assistant professor = 3 bedrooms + 1 sitting room... Nowadays even relative strangers ask each other questions like: Where did you graduate from? Where's your work unit in the pecking order? Does your job give you the status of a vice-department head, department head, vice-bureau chief, or bureau chief? How many rooms in your flat besides a sitting room? Only in a society constructed like a pyramid of pecking orders can you ask questions like that, so specific that they verge on rudeness. No one cares to know about your point of view on a particular subject, or if you have any bold new ideas.

Talking with my brother made me want to cry. He's only eighteen years old. I know he didn't want to talk to me then. His brain is filled with countless useless facts that he thinks will get him a good score on the university entrance exam, but when it comes to matters of the heart he's an emotional blindman.

The next day was Sunday. I got out of bed early and put the family's clothes in the washing machine. Then I sat down on the sofa and put on some music as the washing machine performed its appointed tasks. I love Cesar Franck's organ music. The sound of the organ makes me feel weightless, as if I'm floating in the clouds. The music gradually makes the entire earth, other people, and me all shrink into insignificance; I feel like I want to grab ahold of something, to embrace something solid and real... Whenever I hear a series of noble and distant-sounding melodies, I suddenly feel as if I have committed a crime. I asked myself, why had I begun my experiment with silence? Why couldn't I just say what I wanted to say, and share what was in my heart with the members of my family?

The music stopped suddenly, and I felt like I had fallen out of the sky and crashed to the ground. I noticed my brother's finger, still pointed as he withdrew it from the STOP button on the cassette player, and his angry face as he came up to me and said: "Pain in the ass! Don't interrupt me when I'm memorizing my vocabulary words!"

I leaped up from the sofa, trembling with rage. But my brother had already disappeared into his room.

As I turned back to the washing machine, I could hear my parents engaging in one of their typical "battles of patience". Every two or three days they argue about some trivial matter. They never really get angry at each other, but neither will either of them take the initiative to back off; they just go on bickering with remarkable tenacity. This time it was about a can of sardines they'd just opened. My father insisted the sardines tasted much worse than the last can. My mother thought they tasted exactly the same.

"It's impossible for a canning factory to maintain consistent quality, even in a single batch."

"But they've got quality control."

"Why do they taste so bad then? They stink to high hell."

"It's your taste-buds that stink, you can't even tell the difference."

And so on…

I hung the clothes on the line on the balcony to dry. My mother announced it was time for lunch. Usually we only eat two meals on Sunday. My father and brother took up their usual positions on either side of the table and ate everything except the sardines. Before she sat down, my mother handed me three letters that had been sitting on the cupboard. She'd picked them up when she went downstairs to get the morning paper. She wanted to make sure everyone was watching when she handed them to me. I opened them one by one, spread them out on the table before me, and read them through slowly to the accompaniment of clicking chopsticks and chewing sounds. I was aware of at least two sets of eyes watching me and my letters.

My dear mother and father: All you have to do is ask me sincerely and be willing to tell me exactly what's on your mind, and I'll be more than happy to start talking again...

At that moment an obstinate-sounding voice broke the silence: "Are you going to eat here this afternoon?"

I shook my head, folded up the letters and stuffed them into my pocket.

I spent the afternoon wandering around the bookstores and had dinner in a fast-food restaurant.

By the second week, not speaking became easier for me, and I even began to enjoy it. Long periods of silence can teach you a lot about the world and other people.

On the sixteenth day of my experiment, Lao Zhan handed me the report forms I had turned in two weeks earlier, the ones he had stacked up so neatly on his desk. He said: "There are five blanks here you didn't fill in properly."

He didn't blame me for not having done my work properly, nor criticize himself for not having checked my work earlier, nor did he make an example of my carelessness to teach Miss Peng or my contemporary a lesson. It boiled down to this: I had failed to fill in a few blanks, the reports had been circulated around, and now two weeks later they were back in my hands, and he was asking me to complete them and return them to him.

On day 20, I suffered a major shock. A tragic accident had taken place somewhere in our work unit, resulting in a serious loss of life and property. I learned about it just as I was entering the building and ran into Sangsang. She was all excited and told me that her boyfriend had just decided to devote himself to writing about this event. Everyone was saying that the hottest literary genre now was reportage. Though he wasn't about to give up his "Nearly Transparent Brilliance of the Deep-blue Sky", he wanted to try his hand at the literature of catastrophe.

Naturally this topic came up in our office, but there it was perceived in an entirely auspicious light. Miss Peng said that it reminded her of a mysterious accident that had taken place more than twenty years ago. Though the three people involved in the accident had been standing very close to each other, the one on the left died instantly, the one on the right was permanently disabled, and the one in the middle escaped unharmed — for him it was as if the disaster had not taken place at all. My contemporary surmised that this had something to do with electrical waves emanating from outer space, the same waves that caused the AIDS virus. Lao Zhan made tea, giving each of us equal portions of the Liu'an leaves from Anhui he had just bought, while lecturing us with a sweet smile on his face: "Now that it's all over, there's really nothing we can do about it. I hear some other work units in our network think we should shoulder some of the responsibility, but the bureau leadership refuted all of their claims last night. In order to avoid any misunderstandings, I recommend that none of you discuss this in public for the time being."

When I left the room, slamming the door behind me, they all must have sat there like gaping idiots. No, that's not right. Maybe they just looked at each other and laughed or sighed.

I knocked on the door of the department head's office, but there was no response. I tried the door handle, but it was locked. Then I went to the bureau director's office. I wanted to tell him straight out: From the legal point of view, or in terms of strict executive responsibility, our work unit was probably not responsible for the accident. But if we acknowledged the fact that our work unit is one of several units on the same level that make up a functional system, and that our unit is a key link in this network, then we could hardly afford to be so complacent. We had two choices, either take full responsibility for the accident, or abolish our work unit all together. But that's not all. I'm the first person in our work unit who ought to be blamed for the accident, since it was me who had turned in a pile of incomplete report forms. If these forms had to be turned in on time, then by failing to do so I had committed a serious breach of duty; if the report forms were of negligible importance, then my job should have been abolished a long time ago... I'm sure the bureau chief would appreciate the logic of this. I'm sure he at least browsed through my proposal for reform once... When I opened the door and barged into the bureau chief's room, he was sitting at his huge desk going over some papers. While I stood there in the doorway, he raised his head, and we glanced at each other nervously.

"Haven't you got the wrong room?"

There was no trace of hostility in either his voice or his expression.

I froze from head to toe, and suddenly remembered my vow of silence. "Uh...Uh...Uh...Uh...Uh...," the bureau chief said as he stood up and walked over to a spot two paces away from me. Looking apologetic, he continued, "Oh my oh my oh my, what a terrible memory I have! Aren't you from the...uh...department? One of the activists! Yeah..yeah.. yeah.. I heard you haven't been so active lately... you ought to be a little more lively, eh? Eh? Heh... heh...heh... I've read your proposal for reform, yes indeed, I've read it. You're a model reformer, aren't you? Yes, yes...yes...yes... yes... This is a major period of reform in China, the Central Committee's committed to seeing it through, yes, deeply committed. People like you, all you comrades in the rank and file, especially all of you younger comrades, are full of enthusiasm... full of it. The key burden rests on *all* of our shoulders. If we don't do our part there's bound to be a blockage in the infrastructure."

My heart melted when he said that. If the bureau director had asked me to sit down with him, we could very well have had a wonderful heart-to-heart talk. But he kept us both standing, even though his large well-lit office was furnished with a Belgian-style sofa and a fine chrome and glass coffee table.

"...We've got to liberate people's thinking, and seek truth from facts, right?... Let everyone contribute their own proposals, then we'll all put our heads together. Of course everyone's position in the organization is different, and we've still got to keep an eye on the other departments, and be a little more careful about the way we do things. You young people certainly understand that."

The phone rang, and he wasted no time answering it.

I turned and left the room.

I remained calm and collected during lunch and the rest of the afternoon. See no evil, hear no evil. My silence made me think only about myself.

After work I decided to walk home rather than take the bus. I had a Walkman and was listening to Franck's organ music. My soul was in the clouds. I could feel the earth spinning. Gradually it shrank into a fuzzy blob of colours which faded into the distance and separated into indistinct droplets, a dark blue sky filled with innumerable points of light. I thought about the planet we live on, the community of human animals that inhabits the earth, and all those infinitesimally tiny, suffering, anxious, contrite and helpless egos that make up this community. I felt pity and compassion, which gave me the urge, stronger than anything I'd ever felt in my life, to embrace something real.

My mother had given me three letters on Sunday. I had torn up two of them and kept one. He wanted me to go and see him and talk things out. He was the only man who could turn me on, so maybe with him it was possible to have the kind of conversation I'd been longing for. I'd tried before with other men, but never got very far. Maybe that was because I had some mental blocks about it. He was about to get a divorce but hadn't made a final settlement with his wife yet.

He didn't have a place of his own and was living in a friend's flat. I got a bad scare when I knocked on the door. It seemed he had been waiting by the door ever since he had written that letter to me. As the door shut behind me, he gave me a big bear-hug. I struggled free. He said: "There's no one here, just you and me. No one's going to interrupt us, we can be alone."

He carried me into the room in his arms. The flat was compact and sparsely furnished, but equipped with everything you needed.

He helped me take off my coat and sweater, and hugged me again. He was certainly "something real", a living, breathing, solid entity. I hugged him with all my might. He was the type that excited me sexually. He was lean and muscular, with lots of sharp angles on his body and practically no curves. He had a thick head of hair and a heavy beard, and rarely got haircuts or shaved. The pores of his skin were deep enough to be visible and his blood vessels bulged all over. He smelled of sweat, rather than soap, hair creme, shaving lotion or mothballs. He had broad shoulders and a narrow waist, with powerful pectorals and relaxed neck muscles. His kisses were savage but sincere, his embraces full of confidence and urgency.

I spoke to him with my eyes, reminding him of an earlier promise.

"I wanted to get together with you and talk about my divorce settlement. But that's not necessary now. It's all over, I'm a divorced man, as of this morning. I'm free. I'm all yours. You can enjoy me to your heart's content. And I can enjoy you to my heart's content."

He started to unbutton my shirt. I began to caress his neck, his shoulders... but when I got to his buttons, I stopped and pushed his hand away. He looked at me in surprise.

I looked at him. I thought he might ask: "Why don't you say something?"

But he didn't. He started with his hand again, but I stopped him.

"Don't you feel like it?"

I hardly expected him to say that.

With my eyes, I told him what I wanted. It was all quite simple. Why didn't he ask me if I wanted a glass of water? Or if I wanted to wash my face? Or if I was hungry? Since we were all alone in our little sanctuary, with no obstacles or interruptions, what was the big hurry? We could go slowly, and enjoy every moment of our togetherness. Was our pleasure limited to this one thing?

He failed to understand that. He embraced me again and started to undo my clothing, but I pushed him away.

He stared at me blankly.

I felt a storm brewing inside me. This was a matter of life and death. I didn't expect very much. If he would only say: "Let's sit and talk..."

"Don't you love me?"

I didn't nod my head.

"You don't feel like it?"

I nodded.

He looked pitiful. A macho guy like him should never look so pitiful.

All I wanted was for him to say, plain and simple: "Let's sit down and talk...."

But he folded his arms across his chest and said in typical macho fashion: "I never force anybody."

I buttoned up my blouse and put my sweater back on.

"What's the matter, you want to see my divorce certificate first?"

That broke my heart.

"Why don't you say something?"

Finally he had noticed my silence!

I put my coat on.

Then he rushed at me, grabbed my arm, and shouted into my face:

"Talk! Say something!"

I could feel his hot breath on my face.

I opened my mouth. I desperately wanted to speak to him.

"My god! I don't believe how white your teeth are!"

When he gasped in admiration, I could hear his voice trembling. At that very instant, I wanted him to kiss my white teeth passionately, or say: "Let's sit down and talk…" If he had done either of those things, I would have surrendered to him instantly.

But he pushed me away and said something totally unexpected: "I'm a real loser."

…I was strolling down the street. There were people all around me. I wanted to meet someone with needs like my own, and sit down for a real heart to heart talk. But how could I meet someone like that? No one on the street even looked at me. I stopped in front of a shop window. The shop was closed but the display window was lit up. There were a few mannequins there in fur coats, standing in front of a black velvet background. I could see my reflection in the window: it was like a giant mirror. I opened my mouth wide, and for the first time in my life I noticed how even and white my teeth were. My lips also had a fresh rosy colour. My eyes were shining too. I had bright eyes and shining teeth. Red lips and white teeth. Never before in my life had I felt such profound pity for myself.

A man with bulging goldfish eyes and almost no chin came up to me and whispered: "Got any Foreign Exchange Certificates?"

He made a sign with his hands indicating the rate he was offering.

His teeth were disgusting. I felt nauseous.

"Uhh…you wanna *buy* Foreign Exchange Certificates?" He blinked and made another hand signal.

I turned away and left.

The lights on the long street were rather dim. I could make out a few isolated neon signs in the distance.

I didn't feel like walking any more, and headed for a bus stop.

A girl was coming my way. One glance and I knew she came from the countryside in some remote province. She was wearing a kerchief with a flower print, long out of fashion, and was carrying an overnight bag. I stepped aside to let her pass, but she accosted me.

"Big Sister, help me, please!"

I thought she was going to ask me for money.

But she didn't. She put down her bag and handed me a piece of paper. She had lost her way. I tried to read the address on the paper under the street light. The place was probably in the neighbourhood, but I didn't know how to get there.

I handed the piece of paper back to her and shook my head.

"Help me, please. I'm going crazy trying to find this place. Please, don't make fun of me, like the rest of them."

She came from Sichuan. She was half a head shorter than me. She looked up when she spoke to me, but instead of looking into my eyes, she looked at my mouth. Only people without ulterior motives look at you in that way.

"I came here to work for a family." She handed me a letter. I wasn't really interested but I took it anyway and glanced at it. People who want to hire a maid or baby-sitter who don't trust the "Anhui connection"[2] or the Labour Service Bureau get relatives of

---

[2] Many female domestics in Peking come from Anhui province.

theirs who live in the countryside to send a cousin, sister or aunt to the big city to work for them, certainly the most reliable way to hire a maid. When I noticed that the postmark on the letter was more than six months old, I took a closer look at her.

She took the letter back and said calmly: "I know what you're thinking: Why didn't I come earlier? Why didn't I write first? Why didn't I have them come and get me? Just now a woman told me, maybe they found someone already, and that I should go back home now... You can't imagine how hard it was for me to get here! Where I come from, it's so far away-ooh,[3] so poor-ooh, so backwards... Ooh-there's progress there, but so very slow. Nothing like it is here-ooh. So many electric lights, and so bright and shiny-ooh. Please listen to me, there's lots of things I want to tell you-ooh. Can you imagine-ooh? My third cousin-ooh, he teaches physics in a middle school. He learned physics from a teacher who went to a teachers' college in Chengdu. This cousin of mine taught electronics for many years, taught his pupils about electric lights, telephones, printed circuits, electric motors. Can you imagine, he taught his students from the pictures in the textbook, and what he'd learned from his teacher. But he himself had never seen an electric light. You don't believe me? I wouldn't lie to you-ooh? In 1978 when they first hooked up a power line in our village, my third cousin was sick in bed, very sick. He wanted more than anything to see an electric light working, so he had a line strung to his house, and a light bulb there all ready to go. He just lay there, staring at the light bulb, waiting for the power to be switched on. And the very same day they switched on the electricity, he died, the very same day! That's in the village I come from. I went to middle

---

[3] Sichuanese typically add an "ooh" to the end of a phrase or sentence, something like the English "... you know".

school, I came seventh best in the exams, I read about trains and aeroplanes and skyscrapers in textbooks, but I had never seen them. I knew I had to get away from there... If they have a baby-sitter already, I'll find something else to do, I want to look around, try my luck. Big Sister, help me! Help me!"

I gave her the once over. She was not at all good looking, with long, narrow eyes. Her big rough hands didn't match the rest of her body. But her teeth were extremely white. Some people judge how civilized a place is by the quality of its toilets; in the same way, a person's dental hygiene is one way of judging that person's desire for a better life.

I suddenly felt something frozen in my chest beginning to melt.

"Big Sister, aren't you listening to me?" She then started talking to me in fluent sign language, while she babbled on: "My brother and his wife are deaf and dumb. When we work on our private plot, we talk about everything under the sun-ooh!"

I grabbed her hands tightly.

Her jaw dropped. What I did shocked her. Perhaps this was the first time anyone had behaved that way with her.

My vocal chords, dormant for twenty days, began to stir. A hesitant, crystal-clear voice burst from the depths of my soul:

"How white your teeth are!"

February 1988
Green-leaf Cottage

Translators

Geremie Barmé
  Black Walls
  Zooming in on 19 May 1985

Don J. Cohn
  The Woman With Shoulder-length Hair
  White Teeth

Stephen Fleming and Don J. Cohn
  Bus Aria

Richard Rigby
  The Wish

"Black Walls" was first published in *Renditions* No. 23 (Spring 1985).

"The Wish" was first published in *Renditions* No. 25 (Spring 1986).

"Bus Aria" was first published in *Chinese Literature*, Winter, 1986.

Edited and reprinted with permission.

A